毕淑敏
双语美文

A Bilingual Edition of
Beautiful Stories
by Bi Shumin

U0725847

幸福的七种颜色

The Seven Colours of Happiness

毕淑敏 著

朱虹 刘海明 译

GUANGXI NORMAL UNIVERSITY PRESS
广西师范大学出版社
·桂林·

幸福的七种颜色
XINGFU DE QIZHONG YANSE

出版统筹：张俊显
品牌总监：耿　磊
选题策划：耿　磊
责任编辑：王芝楠
助理编辑：韩杰文
美术编辑：卜翠红　刘冬敏
营销编辑：杜文心　钟小文
责任技编：李春林

图书在版编目（CIP）数据

幸福的七种颜色：汉、英 / 毕淑敏著；朱虹，刘海明
译 . 一桂林：广西师范大学出版社，2020.1
　（毕淑敏双语美文）
　ISBN 978-7-5598-2402-8

　Ⅰ . ①幸… Ⅱ . ①毕…②朱…③刘… Ⅲ . ①散文集－
中国－当代－汉、英 Ⅳ . ①I267

　中国版本图书馆 CIP 数据核字（2019）第 259734 号

广西师范大学出版社出版发行

（广西桂林市五里店路 9 号　邮政编码：541004）
　网址：http://www.bbtpress.com
出版人：黄轩庄
全国新华书店经销
保定市中画美凯印刷有限公司印刷
（保定市西三环 1566 号　邮政编码：071000）
开本：880 mm × 1 350 mm　1/32
印张：6　　字数：120 千字
2020 年 1 月第 1 版　　2020 年 1 月第 1 次印刷
印数：0 001~6 000 册　　定价：39.80 元

如发现印装质量问题，影响阅读，请与出版社发行部门联系调换。

在书中温暖相遇

几年前，广西师范大学出版社出版了我的一套书。在这套书里，我写了自己在遥远西藏的往事，写了当医生的难忘经历，写了担当心理医生时听到的故事和引发的思考……

书是缔造心灵的塑形工具。东方文化中，心并不单单指那个解剖学上的泵血器官，而是汇聚每个人的品格情操的智慧之海。有一颗仁慈之心，会爱世界爱他人爱生活，爱自身也爱大家。有一颗自强之心，会勤学苦练百折不挠，宠辱不惊大智若愚。有一颗尊严之心，会珍惜自然善待万物。有一颗流量充沛羽翼丰满的心，会乘上幻想飞船，抚摸众星的翅膀。

我遇到了朱虹老师，她就是拥有这样一颗多彩之心的睿智长者。很高兴她喜欢我书中的文字。

最初，朱虹老师想挑一些篇章翻译，作为礼物送给远在大洋彼岸的孙女外孙女们珍藏。广西师大出版社的编辑获悉这个想法，郑重邀请朱虹和刘海明老师，将本套书全部翻译出来。

这不是轻易可完成之事，是颇为繁复艰辛的工程。朱虹老师已年近90，是中国社科院德高望重的英美文学研究专家，也是一位把我国很多当代文学作品翻译介绍到国外的杰出翻译家。长期生活在国外的刘海明老师造诣高超文采斐然，和朱虹老师相得益彰珠联璧合。两位老师以醇厚学养和丰富经验，深思熟虑地将这些文字，按照英语思维方式和阅读风格，给予精彩转化，赋予它们以另外一种语言表达的鲜活生命。

补充一个小插曲。我的散文"精神的三间小屋"，被选入2018年教育部审定的全国义务教育语文教科书九年级上册。刘海明老师加班加点，将这篇文章翻译出来，收入本套书，真是雪中送炭。

面对这套双语书，我心中充盈知遇之恩和感念之情，在此向所有付出心血的老师们深表谢意！

人生是砥砺向前且充满顿挫的历程，不时筋疲力尽茫然四顾。这本小书的故事和它的成书过程，让我又一次相信，行程中有不期而至的风雨，更有美好温暖的巧遇。朱虹、海明老师和我在文字中结识，现在，我期待着——我们和你——亲爱的读者，在书中相逢。

之后，让咱们再次充满信心地出发！

2019年11月5日

When We Meet Inside a Book

A few years ago, Guangxi Normal University Press published a collection of my stories. In them, I wrote about the years I spent in remote Tibet, my unforgettable experience working as a physician, and stories and musings I gathered as a counseling psychologist.

Works of literature help shape our heart. In Eastern cultures, the heart is the sea of wisdom that nurtures our character, other than a mere organ anatomically responsible for pumping blood through the body. It is with the kind heart that one loves the world, others and life; love of oneself and all people. It is with the hardy, aspiring heart that one strives on, never giving up, and is wise, artless and unflappable. It is with the dignified heart that one cherishes nature and is kind to all creatures great and small. It is with the heart brimful of confidence that one floats on wings of imagination, touching the stars.

Then I met Zhu Hong, an erudite elder with such an unfailingly rich heart, and was most delighted that she liked the stories of this collection.

Initially, Zhu Hong had planned to translate a selection of them as a gift to be held dear by her granddaughters across the ocean. However, when the editorial staff of Guangxi Normal University Press learned about this, they decided to invite Zhu Hong and Liu Haiming to translate the entire collection into English.

It was no small undertaking, a project requiring much dedication. Zhu Hong, in her late eighties, is a venerated scholar in the field of English and American Literature with the Chinese Academy of Social Sciences. She is also noted for her incomparable translations of outstanding works of modern Chinese literature, bringing them to a wider international audience. Liu Haiming, an accomplished translator having studied and worked extensively abroad, collaborated with Zhu Hong on this project. The two scholar-translators pored over the Chinese texts and managed to bring out the spirit of the original, and give life to the stories in the English language in all its beauty and flexibility.

Incidentally, my essay "Three Little 'Rooms' for Your Soul" was selected for the 2018 edition of the Ministry of Education-approved high school textbook for Chinese Language and Literature, for the first semester of the ninth year of National Compulsory Education. Beavering away, Liu Haiming had it timely translated for inclusion in the present collection.

As this bilingual collection was ready for printing, I felt most grateful for our privileged connection. My thanks go to all who have put all the hard work into its publication.

Life is a journey, with inevitable challenges and setbacks, which, at times, can wear you out, and loneliness captures you. Yet, for all the storms out of the blue, there are also fortuitous, heartening encounters along the way—a belief borne out by the stories in this collection and its publication. Zhu Hong, Haiming and I met in the pages of these stories, and now I look forward to our encounter with you, dear readers, in this little collection.

Then, brimful of confidence again, we will journey on!

Bi Shumin, November 5, 2019

contents
目 录

contents
目 录

学会维持快乐

维持喜悦，是一件需要努力的事情，并不是天性使然。

喜悦与悲哀，都是人之情感的一部分。沉浸在悲哀中是很正常自然的事，如果不是有意识地走出来，人们会深陷悲哀的沼泽中，很久无法自拔。

通常，除了时间以外，我们还需要一个猛醒，一声恫吓，才能从悲伤中振作起来。

喜悦则不是这样，它会像沙漏一样，在不知不觉中渗走，只留下一个回忆的空壳，令人惆怅。

要学会维持你的快乐，这就是不断地感恩，不断地将脸朝向有光的地方。

时间长了，你自然就学会了和喜悦相处的诀窍。

希望你一站出来，就让人能从你身上看到生命的光彩。

生命是有光彩的，如果说一朵山野中的小花都有盈手的清香，一段腐木都会污浊不散，那么，我们的生活，也可以弥散出味道。

期望着你能让你的生命像黑暗中的米兰和雪中的梅，人们还没有走进，就会被熏染，就会深深地吸一口气，不由自主感叹这飞来的一段美妙。

卢梭说：人是生而自由的，却又无往而不在枷锁之中。

我们平日感觉自由的时候甚少，感觉枷锁的时间甚多。不过，仔细想想，你还是自由的。所有的枷锁都是你自己套上的。

打开枷锁享受自由的滋味，有些人从来也没有享受过。他们无所不在地夸大了枷锁的力量，忽略了自己的主动。只有自己才能化解生命故事中那么多的伤痛和矛盾，让自己日趋圆满。

记住，你永远是你自己的主人。

宇宙不公平吗？不啊。宇宙只是漠不关心。

自己的事要自己做。这是幼儿园就教会我们的道理。人们之所以看到很多人在讴歌艰难，是因为那多是成功了的人在自言自语。不要喜欢艰难，不要人为地制造艰难。

其实，艰难是把大部分人的才华磨损了，把大部分人的意志都侵蚀了，把大部分人的幸福耽搁了。我相信，在肥沃的土地上，充满阳光的空气中，才能生长出更多垂着穗子却丰硕饱满的庄稼。

　　那么，快乐是什么？快乐的用处就是——它能使你认识到自己的价值，感受到他人认可了你的成就，你对这个世界是有用的，还有一个附带的可贵用处，就是能让你健康。

Learn to Keep Your Joy

Keeping your joy requires efforts; it is never a matter of natural instinct.

Joy and sorrow are both common emotions. It is only normal and natural for humans to feel at times an abiding sense of sorrow. We need to make conscious efforts to lift ourselves out of grief, lest we should be perpetually mired.

Sometimes, it takes a jolt, a sharp warning, more than time, to get us out of our gloom.

Yet joy, in contrast, may slip away by itself, leaving us crestfallen, with nothing but an empty husk of its memory.

If you want to keep the fountain of joy flowing, be grateful and turn always towards the bright light.

In time, keeping your joy in life will come naturally to you. All in your presence, so I hope, will sense its glow.

Joy is the glint of sunlight in life. If a little alpine bloom can be delightfully fragrant, and a rotting log smell mildew, then life emanates its aroma, too.

I hope that your life can be sweetly aromatic, like the Chinese perfume plant that blooms in the shade or the plum in the snow. Anyone approaching will marvel at its sweetness, inhaling deeply, as it were, in spite of themselves, and feeling its infectious power.

Jean-Jacques Rousseau once said, "Man is born free, and everywhere he is in chains."

We may indeed often feel being in chains and seldom do we seem free. However, come to think of it, we are in fact largely free, and all the shackles are put on us by ourselves.

Some have never had the opportunity to taste freedom, being encumbered by shackles of one kind or another. They exaggerate the power of shackles, while ignoring that of their initiative. It is ultimately only you yourself who can alleviate the burdens of despair and deal with the predicament in life, moving toward a consummate finale.

Remember, you are the master of your own destiny.

The world is so unfair, you bemoan. Well, it isn't unfair, but merely doesn't care.

Always clean up your own mess; that's a lesson we learned in kindergarten. We have heard so many bragging about the hardships they have endured. They are often the ones that have fared well and just can't stop tooting their horns. Never relish hardships — nor should you create them on purpose.

For hardships blunt our creativity, whittle away our willpower and hamper our happiness. Only in fertile soil, and with enough sunlight, can a crop be expected to yield a bumper harvest.

So what is joy? Joy is what we feel when we appreciate our own worth in the world, and sense its recognition in others, too; with its remarkable benefit — keeping us healthy — to boot.

快乐之奖

一位悠闲的老人，守候在闹市区的一条繁华马路上。无数的行人从他身边匆匆掠过，如同群群鸥鸟飞越搁浅的轮船。老人睿智的目光巡视着众人的脸庞，不断地轻轻叹息。偶尔他会走到某位行人的面前，有礼貌地拦住他，悄声地说一句什么话，然后把一样东西塞进那人的手里，微笑着离开。

深夜，老人回到一家俱乐部，对负责人说，我已经对每一个我确认的人，发放了奖金。

这是怎么回事？

原来这家富裕的俱乐部突发奇想，拿出了一大笔钱，委派对人的表情很有研究的专家，到城市最繁华的地带守候一天，由专家判定的每一位快乐的人，会得到一笔奖金。

负责人说，唔，你做得很好。只是，我猜想，那笔钱一定不够吧？

老人说，我连那些钱的一个零头都没有用完。整整一天，成千上万的人经过我面前，但是我能确认快乐的人，只有二十二名。

当我第一次看到这份资料的时候，十分诧异。正常人当中，快乐的人是如此稀少吗？当我带着这团疑问，开始观察周围的时候，才发现，答案果然令人震惊。围绕我们的，多是惆怅的脸、忧郁的脸、焦灼的脸、愤懑的脸、谄媚的脸、悲怆的脸、呆板的脸、苦恼的脸、委屈的脸、讨好的脸、严厉的脸、凶残的脸……

快乐的脸如此罕见，仿佛黄梅季节的阳光。快乐的脸不是孤立无援的面具，在它的后面，是一颗快乐的心在支撑。快乐的奖无法发放，真是一个悲剧。

我期待着有一天，到处是由衷的快乐的欢笑的美好的脸，让那家俱乐部，发奖发得破了产。

A Prize for Happiness

An elderly man stood on the sidewalk of a busy city street, seemingly without a care in the world. Pedestrians scurried past him, like seagulls swooping by a stranded boat. His penetrating eyes roved over passersby's faces, with a sigh now and then. Every so often he would walk up to a person, politely asking for his or her permission and then pressing something into their hands after a quick whisper and grin.

Late in the evening, the old man returned to a clubhouse, reporting to someone in charge, "I have given an award to each qualified person I could find."

What was the game?

09

It turned out to be a scheme cooked up by this club of wealthy members: give each happy person a little prize, to be executed by someone with a knack for recognizing human emotions, in the busiest street of the city on a regular day, out of a tidy sum that the club had set aside.

"Well done," the club chairman chortled. "But surely, the sum wasn't enough to last for a whole day, was it?"

"In fact, I only used a mere fraction of the sum," replied the old man. "Out of the thousands that passed in front of me, I could identify only twenty-two that were truly happy."

I was rather startled when I first came across this story. How could happy people be so rare in any regular crowd of humanity? With this doubt in my mind, I began to observe people around me and my own finding was equally startling. I saw too many faces that suggested melancholy, glum, anxiety, anger, sorrow, lethargy, distress, injustice, fawning, servility, harshness, brutality...

Happy faces were indeed hard to find, like the rare spot of sun in a gloomy season of rain. Happiness is not a mask that you can somehow wear; it glows from within. It was tragic for the old man not to find enough people to give the happiness prize to.

I wish someday we could see delightfully joyous and genuinely happy faces everywhere and the club of the wealthy go bust dispensing its prizes for happiness.

锻造心情

心情好像一种很柔软的东西，经常因为自然界的风花雪月或是人世间的阴晴冷暖，剧烈地波动着，蛛丝般震颤飘荡，无所依傍，哪里用得上"锻造"这样充满了金属音响的词呢？

心情于我们是那样的重要，健康与美丽，如若没有一副好心情，犹如沙上建塔，水中捞月，一切都无从谈起。心情与我们形影不离，不，它甚至比影子的追随还要固守得多。光不存在的时候，影子就藏在深深的阴暗中了。只有心情牢牢黏附在胸膛最隐秘的地方，坚定不移地陪伴着我们。快乐的人，在黑夜中也会绽放出笑容；凄苦的人，即使睡着了，梦中也滴泪。

心情是心田的庄稼，只要心脏在跳动，心情就播种着、活跃着、生长着、更迭着，强有力地制约着我们的生存状态。可能没有爱情，没有自由，没有健康，没有金钱，但我们必有心情。

心情还是我们的收割机呢，如果你懊丧，收获的就是退缩和一事无成。如果你郁郁寡欢，只一味地倾诉苦难，朋友最终会离去，留你孑然面对孤灯。如果你昂扬，希望就永远微茫地闪动，激你前行。如果你百折不挠，生活每一次把你压扁，你都会充满了韧性，幽默地弹跳而起，螺旋向上。如果你向每一丛绿树和鲜花打招呼，它们必会回报你欢笑和芬芳。

如果你渴望健康和美丽，如果你珍惜生命每一寸光阴，如果你愿为这世界增添晴朗和欢乐，如果你即使倒下也面向太阳，那么请锻造心情。它宁静而坚定，像火山爆发后凝固的岩浆，充满海绵状的孔隙坚硬无比，它可以蕴含人生的苦难，但绝不会被困难所粉碎，它感应快乐的时候如丝如弦，体贴人间的每一份感动。它凝重时如锚如链，风暴中使巨轮安稳如磐。它在一次次的淬火中，失去的是杂质，获得的是坚韧。它延展着，包容着，被覆着我们裸露的神经，保护着我们精神的海洋和天空。它是蓝色澄清的内心疆域，在那里栖息着我们永不疲倦的灵魂。

让我们的成品——沉稳宁静广博透明的心情，覆盖生命的每一个清晨和夜晚，从此不再因为外界的风声鹤唳而瑟瑟发抖，不再因世间的荣辱得失而锱铢计较，不再因身体的顿挫不适而万念俱灰，不再因生命的瞬忽飘逝而惆怅莫名……

The Tempering of Our Mood

One's mood is something subtle, subject to swings that are precipitated often by the advent of rain, snow or any of the human foibles. It is capacious and frail, like the wavering and vibrating spider's web, and has nothing to do with the malleable metal.

Yet our mood is critical to our emotional wellbeing, without which we have neither health nor beauty to speak of, and any attempt at enhancing health and looks will be futile. Our mood follows us, much more so than our shadow that disappears as the light fades. Our mood is the shadow within, stubborn and unrelenting. A happy person can smile radiantly even in the darkest hours, while a sad one weeps in his dream.

As long as one's heart doesn't stop beating, one has moods. They rise and grow, like seeds sown in a field, until they dominate our existence. Even though we may be without love, freedom, health, and money, we always have our moods.

You reap what you sow: being remorseful and self-loathing, you recoil and end up accomplishing nothing. Depressed, ceaselessly rambling about your sufferings, you end up friendless and alone. However, if you are enthused and hopeful, you push forward. Dauntless and resilient, you fight with tenacity and good humour when life throws you a curve ball. You are rewarded with verdant green and riotous, fragrant blossoms, if you embrace majestic forests and alpine meadows.

Temper your mood, if you yearn for health and beauty, if you cherish each moment of life,

17

if you wish to add brightness and joy to the world and be optimistic even when you fall. Let it be calm and not shifty, like the solidifying lava, porous yet firm, with copious, absorbent capacity. Resilient, you are not crushed by hardships, despite having your fair share of them. You are keenly touched by the warmth of humanity, like chords coming to life on a zither. Your calm and steadfastness are like the anchor that allows a ship to moor in a storm. Through repeated quenching in the process of tempering, you eliminate the fickleness of nerve and gain resilience and calm. Such equanimity is a mark of emotional wellbeing; your inner world a calm sea and your tireless soul at peace.

Let tranquillity, munificence and clarity fill our life, at each dawn and dusk. Let our heart never quiver at the howling winds, or agonize over worldly gains and losses, or become sad at setbacks and vanquished dreams, or be despondent at the ephemerality of life.

幸福的七种颜色

幸福应该有多少种颜色呢？

说不清。我回答。

大家听了可能有点迷糊，说，你自己既然不知道，为什么又曾说过幸福有七种颜色呢？

在文化中，"七"这个数字有一点古怪。

欧洲人自古以来就格外钟情于"七"这个数字。最早的源头该是古希腊人，许多巧合都和"七"有关。希腊人认为自然界是由水、火、风、土四种元素组成的，而社会的基本细胞是家庭。把完整的家庭细分，是由父亲、母亲和孩子三方组成。再做一次加法，把自然和社会组成的世界统计一下，就有七种基本元素。古希腊人酷爱加法，认为世界的基本图形是正方形、三角形以及完美的圆形，毕达哥拉斯学派就是这一主张的坚定拥趸。你劳神把这些图形的角的数量加起来，哈！也是七。由于太多的东西与神秘的数字七有关，他们造七座坛、献七份祭、行七次叩拜之礼，什么都爱凑个七字。"七大主教""七大美德"，连罪也要数到"七宗罪"。当然，最著名的是神也喜欢七，于是一个星期是七天，第七天你可以休息。

七在佛教里面也是吉祥之数，有七宝、七层浮屠等。中华文化对七也颇有好感，《说文》里面说："七，阳之正。"这个七啊，常为泛指，表明多的意思，又神秘又空灵。

托尔斯泰老人家说，幸福的家庭都是相似的，唯有不幸的家庭，各有各的不幸。我当过多年的心理医生，觉得不幸的家庭都是相似的，唯有幸福的家庭却是各有各的不同。

你可能要说，这不是成心和托尔斯泰抬杠嘛！我还没有落到那种无事生非的地步。你想啊，只有香甜的味道，才可反复品尝，才能添加更多的美味在其中，让味蕾快乐起舞。比如椰蓉，比如可可，比如奶油……丰富的层次会让你觉得生活美好万象更新。如果那底味已是巨咸、巨苦、巨涩，任你再搁进多少冰糖多少香料都顷刻消解，那难耐难忍的味道依然所向披靡，让你除了干呕，再无良策。

早年间我当兵在西藏阿里，冬天大雪封山，零下几十度的严寒，断绝了和外界的一切联系，我们每日除了工作就是望着雪山冰川发呆。有一天，闲坐的女孩子们突然争论起来，求证一片黄连素的苦可以平衡多少葡萄糖的甜（由此可见，我们已多么百无聊赖）。一派说，大约五百毫升百分之五的葡萄糖就可以中和苦味了。另外一派说，估计不灵。五百毫升葡萄糖是可以的，只是浓度要提高，起码提到百分之十，甚至百分之二十五……争执不下，最后决定亲自验证。那时候，我们是卫生员，葡萄糖和黄连素乃手到擒来之物，说试就试。方案很简单，把一片黄连素用药钵细细磨碎了，先泡在浓度为百分之五的葡萄糖水里，大家分别来尝尝，若是不苦了，就算找到答案了。要是还苦，就继续向溶液里添加高浓度的葡萄糖，直到不苦了为止，然后计算比例。临到试验开始，我突然有些许不安。虽然小女兵们利用工作之便，搞到这两种药品都不费吹灰之力，但藏北到内地山路迢迢，关山重重，物品运送到阿里不容易啊，不应这样为了自己的好奇暴殄天物。黄连素碎末混入到葡萄糖液里，整整一瓶原本可以输入血管救死扶伤的营养液就报废了。至于黄连素，虽不是特别宝贵的东西，能省也省着点吧。我说，咱缩减一下量，黄连素只用四分之一片，葡萄糖液也只用四分之一瓶，行不行呢？

我是班长，大家挺尊重我的意见的，说，好啊。有人想起前两天有一瓶葡萄糖，里面漂了个小黑点，不知道是什么杂物，不敢输入病人身体里面，现在用来做苦甜之战的试验品，也算废物利用了。

试验开始。四分之一片没有包裹糖衣的黄连素被碾成粉末（记得操作这一步骤的时候，搅动得四周空气都是苦的），兑到一百二十五毫升浓度为百分之五的葡萄糖水中。那个最先提出以这个浓度就可消解黄连之苦的女孩率先用舌头舔了舔已经变成黄色的液体。她是这一比例的倡导者，大家怕她就算觉得微苦，也要装出不苦的样子，损害试验的公正性，将信将疑地盯着她的脸色。没想到她大口吐着唾沫，连连叫着，苦死了，你们千万不要来试，赶紧往里面兑糖……我们为自己"以小人之心度君子之腹"感到羞惭，拿起高浓度的糖就往黄水里倒，然后又推举一个人来尝。这回试验者不停地咳嗽，咧着嘴巴吐着舌头说，太苦了，啥都别说了，兑糖吧……那一天，循环往复的场景就是女孩子们不断地往小半瓶微黄的液体里兑着葡萄糖，然后伸出舌尖来舔，顷刻抽搐着脸，大叫，苦啊苦啊……

直到糖水已经浓到了几乎要拉出黏丝，那液体还是只需一滴就会苦得让人打战。试验到此被迫告停，好奇的女兵们到底也没有求证出多少葡萄糖能够中和黄连的苦味。大家意犹未尽，又试着把整片的黄连素泡进剩下的半瓶里去，趁着黄连素还没有融化，一口吞下，看看结果如何。这一次很快得到证明，没有融化的黄连之苦，还是可以忍受的。

把这个试验一步步说出来，真是无聊至极。不过，它也让我体会到，即使你一生中一定会邂逅黄连，比如生活强有力地非要赐予你极困窘的境遇，比如你遭逢危及生命的重患必得要用黄连解救，比如……你都可以毫无惧色地吞咽黄连。毕竟，黄连是一味良药啊！只是，千万不要人为地将黄连碾碎，再细细品尝，敝帚自珍地长久回味。太多的人习惯珍藏苦难，甚至以此自傲和自虐，这种对苦难的持久迷恋和品尝，会毒化你的感官，会损伤你对美好生活的精细体察，还会让你歧视没有经受过苦难的人。这些就是苦难的副作用。苦的力量比甜的力量要强大得多，不要把黄连碾碎，不要让它嵌入我们的生活。

只要你认真寻找，幸福比比皆是。幸福不是一种颜色，也不是七种颜色，甚至也不是一百种颜色……幸福比所有这些相加还要多，幸福是无限的。

The Seven Colours of Happiness

How many colours does happiness have?

"I can't exactly tell," I'd reply.

Bamboozled, you may pursue, "Why then did you once say happiness has seven colours?"

Well, let me begin with the number seven, which has peculiar cultural meanings.

The Europeans have long been fascinated with the number seven. The ancient Greeks came up with the concept of the four basic elements — earth, water, air, and fire — to explain the forces of nature, and the notion of the father, mother and child as the basic tripartite social unit. Altogether, they are the seven elements that make up the natural and social world. The ancient Greeks, the Pythagoreans for example, also worked with the basic planar shapes of square, triangle and the perfect circle in the development of Greek geometry. If you take the trouble to add up all their corners, there you are: you have the magic seven. Seven became a sacred number for so many mystic rituals. There were biblical stories of "building seven altars," "offering a sacrifice of seven bulls and rams," and "bowing down seven times..." all rounding up to seven. Then there were "the seven great bishops," "seven heavenly virtues", and "seven deadly sins." Even the most widely known deity favoured the number seven. Thus we end up having the seven-day week, with the seventh day set aside as the Sabbath.

Seven is also an auspicious number in Buddhism, with the Seven Treasures, the seven-level pagodas, etc. In ancient Chinese cultural symbolism, seven represents a positive, south-facing orientation. All in all, the number seven connotes multiplicity, with a mystic hint.

Leo Tolstoy famously wrote, "All happy families are

alike; each unhappy family is unhappy in its own way." With my years of clinical experience as a counselling psychologist, I would rather believe the reverse to be true: All unhappy families are alike; each happy family is happy in its own way.

This sounds a bit like nitpicking with Tolstoy, you may say. Well, I am that petty and quarrelsome for no reason. What I intend to say is that when life is good, it is rich with myriad flavours, like a tantalizing fare made with delightful ingredients such as grated coconut, cocoa, cream… teasing your taste buds and making them dance like seaweed. However, if life is sad, it will be void of all sweet flavours, like an overly salted dish, unpalatable and provoking disgust, no matter how much sweetener or condiments you add when cooking it.

Back in my days as an army medic in Ngari, Tibet, we would spend much of our time, when not working, staring blankly at the snowy mountains and glaciers. For all road access was cut off in winter because of heavy snowfall and temperatures plunging well below minus twenty Celsius. One day, the dawdling girls had a heated debate on how much glucose would be needed to mitigate the bitterness of one Berberine tablet (You can see how bored we were then). One camp argued for five hundred millilitres of 5% Dextrose solution, while the other a higher concentration of at least 10%, or even 25%. No one could be convinced, so we decided to put different solutions to a test. We were all medics and glucose and Berberine tablets were literally at our fingertips. We put our scheme to work right away. The plan was simple: one Berberine tablet was to be ground to a fine powder and dissolved in a 5% Dextrose solution. Each of us would taste it. If it were no longer bitter, then we'd have our answer. Otherwise, we would keep adding glucose until it was not bitter and the exact level of concentration would be worked out. However, as we set to work, I grew uneasy. Although we could easily get the samples, it would be unseemly to put them to waste to satisfy our curiosity. For all the medical supplies we had in northern Tibet had to be trucked over long, treacherous mountain roads from the depot on the plains. A bottle of Dextrose solution that could otherwise be used in healing or life-saving transfusion would be made useless when tainted with Berberine powder. As for the Berberine tablet, even though it wasn't terribly valuable, we still should minimize our use. So, I suggested, "Let's be sparing: only one quarter of a Berberine tablet and one quarter of a bottle of the glucose solution, okay?"

Everyone concurred. They respected my suggestion, for I was the leader of the medics' team. One of the girls offered a bottle of glucose solution left unused from two days ago because of a tiny speck of something black floating in it. It could not be used on any patient, and thus came in handy for our experiment.

So it went: one quarter of the Berberine tablet was crushed to powder (there was a whiff of bitterness in the air as we pounded away) and added to 125 millilitres of 5% Dextrose solution. The girl who first suggested such a concentration first tasted the mixture, now turned yellow, with the tip of her tongue. All eyes were riveted on her face; half suspecting that she might cheat by pretending it was no longer bitter, since it was her bet. To our surprise, she blurted, "Glucose, add more. It's so bitter; don't you even try," while spitting out what was on her tongue. We felt ashamed of our pettiness in doubting her objectivity earlier and hastened to add more glucose. Another girl was selected to taste the yellow solution. Again, she blurted, her mouth twitching and her tongue sticking out, because of the awful taste, "It's so bitter. Just add sugar…"

So it went on, with more glucose being added to the one-quarter-filled bottle, each time followed by a tasting and the bleating of "so bitter" out of a crooked face, until the solution became almost gooey saccharine. Yet, the bitterness still sent shivers down the spine of anyone who dared to taste it. The experiment was aborted; leaving us dangling in the dark as to how much glucose could cancel out the bitterness of a quarter tablet of Berberine. Unsatisfied, one girl made a final attempt: gulping down the remaining unused solution, with a whole Berberine tablet added to it. It was established that the bitterness of a Berberine tablet not dissolved was tolerable.

In retrospect, the experiment was utterly frivolous in its boring detail. It taught me, however, while one could ingest Berberine tablets as a proven course of healing or lifesaving therapy, one should never take them after breaking them up or pounding them to powder. In the same vein, refrain from endlessly nursing your bitterness, or forever licking your own wounds. Such a self-important and sadistic tendency to dwell on one's past hardships can be toxic; a negative side effect of suffering. It will impede your appreciation of beauty in life, turning you into a bigot, prejudiced against those who have not had any trials and tribulations in life. Bitterness can be stronger than sweetness. Don't let it take hold of your life.

If you try hard enough, you will find happiness everywhere you look. Happiness is not monochrome, nor does it have only seven colours, or even a hundred colours for that matter. Happiness can be boundless, infinite in its colours.

慈悲

    "慈"在字典上的意思是"和善"。当我们轻轻地念出"慈"的时候，心中会涌起感动。会想起慈母手中长长的丝线，会想到父亲远去的背影。我们还会想到慈眉善目，想到慈祥和慈悲……

    悲是人的七情之一，指痛彻心扉的哀伤，也包含着怜悯和凄凉，比如，悲歌悲剧悲欢离合……

    当慈和悲这两个字连在一起的时候，就发生了奇妙的变化。你会发现它们都以一颗心做底。古人造字是很讲究的，他们在这两个字中注入了自己的体验，也期待着所有喜欢这两个字的人，都会共鸣和震撼。

如果一个人把自己的财富拿出来帮助别人，就等于伸出了自己结实的臂膀，因为劳动者的每一分钱都是他用双手换来的。如果一个人把自己的时间拿出来帮助别人，就等于馈赠出了自己生命的一部分。因为生命是由时间组成的。如果一个人把自己的血液和骨髓捐献出来帮助别人，那么这个人的一生就超越了自我，被放大成人类最美丽的故事，成为一种充满勇敢和友爱的慈悲。

让我们携起手来，用我们的劳动，用我们的时间，用我们的血脉和生命，化作春风，让人间温暖。

Compassion

The Chinese expression for "compassion" consists of two separate characters (ci-bei). The first character indicates "kindness." As we say it softly, we feel a rush of tenderness, being put in mind of the kindly mother sewing, the lone figure of a father going away. We think of all the kindly faces, of benevolence and forbearance...

The second character conveys the notion of "pity," an aching sorrow felt for the sufferings of others. It can be combined with various other characters to separately mean eulogy, tragedy or sadness at parting...

The two characters forming the word "compassion" are

both written with the same bottom half component, or radical, meaning "heart." Our ancient forebears were very particular with the composition of these characters, infusing them with their sense and sentimentality, expecting them to strike a chord with anyone who came to appreciate their power.

When a hardworking man splits his earnings to help others, he shares with them the fruits of his toil, because each penny has been earned by the sweat of his brow. When someone spends his time to help others, he shares with them his life; life that is woven with minutes and hours. When someone gives his blood or bone marrow to help others, he transcends the mere ego, his life becoming emblematic of humanity's goodness, potent of courage and compassion.

Let us join hands in creating better communities of fellowship infused with warmth, using our labour and time — slivers of our life.

假如我出卷子

今天，老师布置的数学作业是：假如我出卷子……让每人给自己的同桌设计一张考卷。

小依拿出一张格纸，方兵问，你见过带格子的卷子吗？卷子都是大白纸的。说着张开两臂比画，好像他是一只大鸟。

小依说，那么大的纸是糊窗户用的，我们家可没有。

下午方兵到校时，递给小依一张雪亮的硬纸说，这是理光复印机专用纸，我爸那儿有的是。

小依说，多好的纸，可以做精美的贺年卡呢。

方兵用手指甲弹弹纸，你要喜欢，我给你一沓。不过你的题要出得容易点，让我也过一次得一百分的瘾。

小依撇嘴，一百分有什么了不起，我都得腻了。她真喜欢那种美丽的纸，所以嘴上才这样说。

方兵说，别吹牛！这回我让你得不成一百分。他找出一本《数学奥林匹克大全》，是表哥从上海寄来的，学校里谁都没有这本书。方兵认真地抄下一道又一道难题，还仔细记下了答案，因为这次出卷子的人，要做一次真正的老师，还得判卷子呢！

小依很守信用，她给方兵出了一张很简单的卷子，方兵第一次得了一百分。他想，如果小依哭丧着脸来找我问答案，我就把那本珍贵的《数学奥林匹克大全》送给小依，反正自己留着也没用。

小依只得了六十分，这还是方兵高抬贵手了呢！可是小依始终没找方兵问过正确答案，每天托着腮帮子想啊想。不知道的人，还以为小依牙疼了。

市里组织统一考试，题目很难，方兵突然眼前一亮，仿佛在拥挤的马路上遇见了熟人，有几道题，正是他给小依出过的，答案他还记得呢！

可老师只给了方兵六十分，说他的答案只是干巴巴的几个数字，完全没有中间步骤，好比是问你鱼是怎样从大海里捞上来的，你却直接拎来了几条咸鱼干，这怎么行呢?

小依得了一百分，可她总像有心事的样子。

If I Were to Design an Exam Paper

The assignment in the maths class that day was to each design exam questions for our desk-mates.

Seeing Xiaoyi taking out a sheet of grid paper, Fang Bing quipped, "Why, nobody puts exam questions on grid paper. You have to use a large plain sheet." Saying which, he stretched his arms to indicate the size of the paper, as if a large bird spreading its wings.

"Those large sheets of paper are for window covering. I don't have them at home anymore," Xiaoyi retorted.

So, when Fang Bing came back from home after lunch, he showed Xiaoyi a glossy sheet of cover stock paper, saying, "This is a special kind of paper for Ricoh photocopiers. My dad has tons of them."

"Such nice paper! Good for making greeting cards," Xiaoyi marvelled.

Tapping the paper with his fingernail, he said, "I can give you a whole ream, if you like it. But you have to promise to write easy questions for me so that I can get a full score for maths for once."

"What's so special about a full score?" Xiaoyi pouted. "I am tired of getting full scores all the time." She was smitten by the beautiful paper, though feigning indifference.

"You needn't brag about it! I will make sure you are not getting a full score this time," Fang Bing shot back. He fished out a copy of *A Complete Collection of Maths Olympiad Sample Questions* that his cousin had sent him from Shanghai. He knew no others in the school had a copy. He began copying down some of the toughest questions, one after another, with notes on correct answers jogged down for himself. We were also to score the answer sheet afterwards, as our maths teacher usually did, for the exam questions we had developed.

Xiaoyi kept her word and designed an exam paper with rather simple questions. Fang Bing got a full score for the first time as he had wished. He thought that he would give Xiaoyi his copy of *A Complete Collection of Maths Olympiad Sample Questions*, if she were to come asking, sheepishly and in gloom, for the correct answers to those tough questions. He had little use for the book any more.

Xiaoyi got a sixty percent, and this was because Fang Bing had been lenient and didn't include all the toughest questions. She never went to him for the answers though. She racked her brains all day to crack the unsolved problems, propping up her chin in her hands. To others not in the know, she looked as if she was bothered by toothache.

Later at a municipal maths exam, participants were given very tough questions to work on. Fang Bing instantly recognized some of the questions, which hit his eye like a firework display — they were the same as those he had given Xiaoyi, the answers to which he still remembered!

However, he only got a score of sixty percent, for he merely put down the final answers without spelling out his calculation. It was like showing up with a few salted herrings when you were asked to explain how fishermen fish. It just wouldn't pass muster.

Xiaoyi got another full score; yet she looked, as always, as though she was musing over something.

鞋带儿

鞋可以分成两大类，有带儿和没带儿的。没带儿的鞋，穿起来方便，可跑不快。有带儿的鞋，穿起来费事，要弯下腰来系鞋带儿。可鞋带儿能把鞋和脚紧紧地固定在一块儿，好像焊锡的作用。人穿着系了鞋带儿的鞋，办事走路就利索多了。那平添的机敏与速度，就蕴含在小小的鞋带儿里面。

我小的时候不怕黑，不怕大的声响，但最恐惧的一件事，就是系鞋带儿。那时上全托的幼儿园，刚开始是老师给系鞋带儿。我觉得这是世上最精巧的活儿，大人们的手指像变魔术似的，三缠两绕，就打出一个黑蜘蛛的结。老师一边打结一边说，叫你们的家长甭买带带儿的鞋，怎么又买来了？一副很劳累的样子。于是，我认定系鞋带儿是个苦活儿。

我决定自己学着系鞋带儿。我费了很长时间学打那个神秘的结。我先是把它拆开，这是很容易的一件事。但拆开之后完全不知道怎样再扭结到一块儿，我第一次明白了破坏一件东西是很简单的，要恢复它就复杂多了。要想靠毁坏某物来学会建造它，实在是很危险、很艰难的事，不是不可以一试，是机会只有一次。

我只好再去找老师。她嘟囔了一句，一个女孩子还这么淘，把鞋带儿都蹬开了。然后飞快地打了个宝贵的结。我目不转睛地看着她粗大的手指像掏耳朵眼儿似的比画了两下，那两根原本孤立的小黑蛇就死死地粘在一起了。

我觉得我记住了那个过程。我又勇敢地第二次拆开了那个结。我费了很长的时间练习，蹲在地上，直到头晕眼花。我用老师的打法却打不成同样的结，只好试验其他新奇的打结法，结果要么完全不是一个结，鞋带始终是两根毫不相干的面条；要么就是它们纠结得太紧密，像个破不出的谜语。面对死结，我用牙齿去咬。鞋带儿的滋味是微咸的，好像话梅。

我很想把自己的过失永远地掩盖过去。可是不行，午睡的时候我脱不下鞋，上不了床，只有带着死结去见老师。她粗暴地说，你怎么这么笨？连鞋带儿都不会解！

我至今不明白，为什么老师看不出，我是在练习一件新本领的时候失败了，却认定我是在重复一个旧过程时的愚蠢？

她的确是费了很大劲儿才解开了死结，有一瞬，她气得几乎要找剪子剪断它们。那一刻，我好害怕而且伤心，我觉得是我害了鞋带儿。

我真正学会系鞋带儿，是在偶然间看到老师给别的小朋友操作这一过程时。我恰好站在老师的背后，一切都那么清晰明朗。我不知道应该算是自己太笨还是老师考虑得不够周到：平日她给我们系鞋带儿，都是蹲在我们的对面，而要学会某项技艺，你必须和老师站在同一方向。

我终于打出了一个惟妙惟肖的结，甚至比老师打的结还要紧，把脚背都勒疼了。我把脚翘得高高的，仿佛要把经过我面前的人都绊一个跟头。鞋带儿快乐地耸立着，等着人们发现这一惊人的事件。但是可惜得很，无论我怎样暗示，大家都不表示惊奇。我只有到老师那里去毛遂自荐，我想就算别人都拿这件事不当回事，我的老师应该由衷地高兴。别的不说，起码她以后不用辛辛苦苦地为我系鞋带儿了。

老师看了我的鞋带儿一眼，又看了我一眼，说，你早就该会了。

我立刻从成功之后的喜悦坠入冰河。我至今感谢我这位老师，她使我幼小的时候就懂得了，有时候你自以为十分辉煌的成就，在别人眼里是理所应当的平淡。

当我学会系鞋带儿以后，我就不再珍惜这个技巧。系鞋带儿很要紧的一条是两个端头要留得一样长。我渐渐地不再像初学那样将它们比画得如孪生兄弟，而是敷衍地一长一短随便绾两个结，任凭它们像断了一只翅膀的蝴蝶在我的鞋面上乱颤。

学会了偷工减料，我很高兴，但鞋带儿开始反击。那个冬天，风寒冷得如同冰糖葫芦上亮脆的薄片，把人的手割出细碎的血口。我刚上学，要走很远的路。未系牢的鞋带儿像风筝飘带，挂在一块尖锐的石头上，那个大马趴摔得我脑浆至今还乱成一团。我懵懵懂懂地爬起来，一时都不明白自己为什么要匍匐在这儿乘凉。好在那截鞋带儿并不忙着隐藏罪责，很招摇地在风中摆动着，让我刻骨铭心地记住它的重要。

不管我多么仇视它，我还是乖乖地将它重新系牢。冷空气把我的指关节变得同蜡烛一样硬，那个漫长的过程，比我一生用过的全部鞋带儿加起来还要长。

从此，我再不敢忽视系鞋带儿这一类的小事。你疏忽了它，它绝不会疏忽了你。你若不信，它就在你最扬扬得意的时候轻轻抖出一个花样，让你静静地躺在大地上清醒。

鞋带儿会断。断了的鞋带儿可以接起来，但接起来的鞋带儿就大不如从前了。首先是它不好使，接头会在每一个穿孔的部位疙瘩着不肯前进。再者是它不结实，会在你最需要登攀的时候突然断裂，让你觉着自己的脚似乎在那一刹突然脱落。

所以鞋带儿断了，我从不将就。别的都可补，鞋带儿不可补，赶快换新的。要赶路，结实最重要。

细细想，"鞋带儿"这个词挺妙。它是鞋子的带子，有了它，你就可以时刻把鞋带在身边。

有的时候，我们跑得不快，只是因为我们没把鞋带儿系好。或许，那原本就是一双没带儿的鞋。

Shoelaces

Shoes come in two kinds — with or without shoelaces. The latter is easy to slip in, yet you can't run fast in them, while the former requires a little effort to put on. You stoop and tie the shoelaces so that your shoes are fastened to your feet. Rambling about or running errands in such shoes, you feel that you and your shoes are one and that you are nimble and ready to roll. You gain speed and efficiency with the good old shoelaces.

Back when I was in boarding preschool, I was never afraid of darkness or strange loud noises, but was terrified of tying my shoes. A houseparent at first tied our shoes for us, which looked to me like the most intriguing magic in the world. With a quick looping and pulling, she could create a neat knot that looked like a black spider. While at it, she would grunt wearily, "I told your parents not to buy shoes with shoelaces. Why are you still wearing these?" This made me believe that tying shoelaces was rather bothersome.

I decided to learn to tie my shoes by myself. It took me a long time; learning to tie the mysterious, awe-inspiring knots. I first undid a knot, which was rather easy. Yet I was totally at a loss as to retying it. I learned for the first time that it is far easier to take something apart than to put it back together. It is risky and difficult to learn to construct something by destructing it first. You only have one chance.

I had to go to the houseparent for help. She grunted before tying the "bunny ears" in a wink, "You pesky little elf. How did you get your shoelaces all undone?" My eyes were riveted on her thick fingers that, with a few quick turns, fastened both ends of the black shoelaces together, swift as a shadow.

I thought I had memorized the trick. Elfishly, I undid the knots again and then kept trying to tie them, in a crouching posture, until I felt dizzy and my vision went blurry. Using the houseparent's method, I couldn't get the same knots. So I fumbled with other knots I invented, which either failed to fasten the shoelaces or made a knot that was frustratingly knotty, like an unsolvable riddle. I used my teeth to loosen a knot that refused to come undone but to no avail and the shoelace, now wet with the dribble, tasted like the salted dried plum.

I tried to hide my knotty problem. But after lunch, I had to go to the houseparent again with my stubborn knots — I couldn't get into the cot for my nap with the shoes on. She scolded me harshly: "You can't even undo your shoelaces? How dumb you are!"

I still don't understand why she would scoff me for my clumsiness, and not cheer my attempt at learning a new skill.

For a moment, the knot even wouldn't budge in her hands. She was ready to give up and resort to the scissors. I felt so horrid, thinking miserably that my clumsiness had put the poor shoelace in peril.

I eventually learned to tie the bunny ears after I observed the houseparent tying the shoes of my playmate. I happened to be standing behind her and it all became plain and clear. I had the same perspective as that of the instructor, which is crucial for learning the new skill, rather than in an opposite position, as was the case when she tied my shoes. I didn't know if I should blame my own dumbness or the lack of consideration on the part of the houseparent for my earlier stumbles.

At long last, I managed to tie the perfect knot, only a bit too tightly, more so than the houseparent would. It felt as though the shoelaces were cutting into the arches of my feet. I tilted the tip of my feet up, as if secretly wishing to trip someone, the bunny ears perking proudly, waiting for admiration. Regrettably, nobody noticed my marvellous feat, despite the screaming hints I dropped. I went to the houseparent who I thought would be most delighted, even though everyone else ignored my success. For at the very least, she wouldn't have to tie my shoes anymore.

Yet after a quick glance at me and my shoelaces, she merely said, "You should have learned this long ago."

This plunged me from bliss to icy gloom. Yet, I am still grateful to the houseparent, for she taught me at an early age that what you regard as an extraordinary accomplishment can be totally mundane in others' eyes.

Once I had learned to tie my shoes, I stopped making a thing of it. I also stopped trying to make both ends the same length so that the knot would look perfectly balanced. I would casually make two loops, often one being larger than the other, wrapping them around each other and pulling to form an uneven knot, like a butterfly of lopsided wings.

I was smug about my little corner-cutting. But shoelaces fought back with a vengeance. In the winter after I had started elementary school, the blustering winds left my hands chapped, as though they had been cut by thin shards of ice. I had to walk a long distance to school and my shoelaces, not properly tied, got snagged on a rock. The spectacular fall made my head swim, and has affected, as I believe, my lucidity to this day. I struggled to get on my feet after wondering for a moment why I was chilling out there in that perfectly horizontal posture. Then the shoelaces that didn't bother to hide their complicity caught my eye. Their importance was etched in my mind forever.

I carefully tied my shoelaces again, no matter how resentful I was. My knuckles were stiff, hardened like wax from the cold. It took forever to get the two knots tied, longer than it would have taken for tying all the shoelaces I ever had in my life.

I have since learned never to be negligent of seemingly trifle matters such as tying my shoes properly. Otherwise, they would make you stumble as you are puffed up with pride and leave you sprawled pensively on the ground.

The shoelace can snap, too. Even though you may tie a knot to fix it, it will never be the same. It can get stuck as you pass it through an eyelet, or may snap again, just as you are in the middle of a tricky climb, causing you to perilously lose your foothold.

Thus, I would never make do with a broken shoelace, and would simply replace it with a spare and move on. I mend anything but never a shoelace. It has to be solid and strong.

And now I think of it, shoelaces are really pivotal to your shoes, without which they simply cannot do their job as they are supposed to.

Sometimes, we cannot run fast enough simply because we haven't tied our shoes properly, or are in ones without shoelaces.

"未来"和"将来"的区别

"未来"和"将来",意思好像差不多。老祖宗是很讲究词语的,比如"秀丽"和"漂亮",都是形容好看,其中有细微却不容忽视的区别。秀丽更自然天成,漂亮则带有人工斧凿的痕迹。那么"未来"和"将来"的差异究竟在哪儿?坦率地讲,我成天和文字打交道,很长时间内搞不清。

原认为"未来"和"将来"的不同,主要在于时间距离的长短。比如常说"走向未来",指比较遥远的时间段,无法改成"走向将来"。换后者也可勉强成文,终不伦不类。也就是说,"将来"似乎是比较贴近眼前的时间，"未来"的尺度则更宏大一些，有点儿像"公里"和"海里"的关系。察觉失误源于听天气预报。播音员常说："在未来二十四小时内……"

一昼夜并不遥远，但这句话不便改成"在将来二十四小时内"。看来单是距此时此刻的时间尺度，并不是这两个词的分水岭。

查词典。

"将来"——"时间词。现在以后的时间。"

"未来"——"就要到来的。指时间。"

如此解释，半斤八两，不了了之。似乎也不便埋怨撰写词典的人敷衍了事，这两个词，在日常使用上，像通用电脑的内存条，置换方便。比如说，"未来是青年人的"，可以很利索地转化为"将来是年轻人的"，理解上无重大歧义。

那么，智慧的老祖宗，为什么还要分得这么细？

近读一本学者的书，茅塞顿开。文中说，"未"字的古义是"滋味"。"未"字和"木"字很相像，比木多了一横。这一横可不是随便加的，有深意。它代表树叶，表示枝干繁茂。繁茂了和滋味有什么关系？此刻需要一点儿艺术想象力——叶子多了说明树木生长情形良好，结的果子就多，味道就好……叶子遮挡了光线，树下就显出朦胧昏昧的样子，表达一种不可知和不可测的神秘性。

哈！原来"未"的意思是——"朦胧的果实"。

至于"将来"的"将"字，居然有些热腾腾的血腥气藏在内里，指"手执利剑屠宰杀生"，所以最初多用于将军和厨师，后来渐渐衍生出"掌握"和"选择"的意思。

如果一定要概括"将"字形象，我愿意把它描绘成遮掩着某些利益的黑色斗篷。

学者说，"未来"是指在我们视野之外的明天，"将来"是指在我们掌握之中的明天。

它们都犀利地指向明天。"未来"是一颗雾蒙蒙的核桃，"将来"是一只隐蔽的魔柜。

某学生成绩优异，人们说，这孩子将来能上重点中学，将来能上大学。在这里，"将来"有一种探囊索物的笃定、运筹帷幄的安详。一个人发了财，只要经营得当，不犯法，他将来会成为富翁。当然意外也随伺左右，如果学生临场失常、考试砸锅，商人徇私舞弊、作奸犯科，人们会说，看！他把自己的将来给毁了。"将来"虽然是预计，在这里却几乎成了人人可以把握的既定事实。

"将来"所说的明天，实质上更多的是一种惯性，是在基础上搭盖的二层楼，是箭已离弦，从铁弓到靶心的飞行过程。于是就有了世故和因循的气息，成了可以预期红利的股票。

　　"未来"更富于冒险和挑战。它是昏暗中的不倦探索，是勇气和智慧的多次叠加战胜了恐惧后的欣喜，是漂浮着幻想泡沫的鸡尾酒。

　　当人们反复强调未来不是梦的时候，内心确知未来有太多梦幻的成分；当人们允诺未来的寰球是和平世界时，面对的是眼前的硝烟和核弹；当人们说，未来要到星际旅行，等待人类的实际上是艰巨拼搏和献身。人们大胆地对未来做出的种种预测，其实只是孤独和勇敢地对着茫茫宇宙的悲壮自白。

　　"将来"很实惠，"未来"多虚幻。一个人在明天的早饭还没着落的时候，考虑的只能是"将来"。但两相比较，我还是更喜欢"未来"的含义。

　　"将来"当然重要。这条优质纱巾，把某些已露端倪的矛盾遮盖着，掩藏起短兵相接的锋芒。温暖地包裹鸡蛋，把它孵化，某个黎明，嘹亮的鸡啼把主人唤醒。一颗海椰被风暴冲到适宜生长的岸边，便会长成大树，需要的仅仅是时间。定时炸弹埋在土里，秒针无声走动，一个惊天动地的时刻渐渐迫近……"将来"不是无源之水、无本之木，"将来"是春种秋收勤劳敬业的农夫。

你播下的是龙种，收获的就不是跳蚤。

　　所以对待将来，如同守候性能可靠的生产线，按部就班是它的最大特征。输进原料，就准备照单接收产品。出了废品，切勿埋怨客观，必是某个环节出了故障，隐患早趴暗处了。如果得到嘉奖，也不必大喜过望，所有数据已经输入，就像火箭发射，飞上蓝天才是正理，凌空一炸就是大冷门了。

　　所以，"将来"的基调是冷静的古朴之色。循序渐进是经，成竹在胸是纬。所以让我们生出些许畏惧、些许忐忑，概因时间的关系。好像正在显影的照片，虽然一切已经定型，毕竟最后一道工序尚未完成。在某些情形下，"将来"之手有足够的力量，把事情变糟。

　　我们永不能对"将来"掉以轻心。

　　但从人类的发展史来说，更重要的是面向未来。猿从树上降落到草地，直立行走，绝不仅仅是已知行为方式的延伸和把握，而是充满了想象力度的空前变革。前景如何，无法预报。最初的人类，只是在若明若暗的曦光中走着，艰难困窘地挺进远方。然而，一个伟大的新世纪，就在这蹒跚的脚印中爆发。

"将来"是沉稳的，"未来"是炙烈的。"将来"是简明扼要的，"未来"是华美铺张的。"将来"是务实的，"未来"是缥缈的。"将来"是有条不紊的，"未来"是浮想联翩的。"将来"是殚精竭虑的，"未来"是高瞻远瞩的。"将来"是惨淡经营的，"未来"是举重若轻的。"将来"是可以揭秘、一览无余的苫布，"未来"是永在夜空闪烁、不可触及的星巢。

　　"将来"更多地属于个体。"未来"则是全人类远眺的家园。

　　现今的人们，常常为自己设计多种"将来"，将来变得越来越精确和细致。但一己的将来固然重要，整个人类的未来，更是现代人必须关注的方向。"将来"和"未来"结合在一起，就是飞翔的魔毯，把我们载往远方的树林，那里有朦胧的新的果实。

"In Future" and "In the Future"

"In future" and "in the future" may seem quite similar. Yet, there are fine differences not to be overlooked — differences that our ancient forebears were particular about when they first created the Chinese script, as they did with "beauty" and "prettiness," for example. The former implies something natural while the latter makeup and contrivance. What then is the difference between "in future" and "in the future?" To be honest, I had been baffled for a long time, though supposedly I was something of a wordsmith.

At first, I thought their key difference lay in the variance of future time. "In Future" may indicate some time in the immediate future, while "in the future" vaguely distant, as in the case of "make more progress in the future." Then I realized I wasn't being very precise, after I had heard the weatherman using "in the future" when referring to "in the next 24 hours…" Thus, it looked as though the duration of future time is not the key.

So I consulted a dictionary which says that in future means "from now on" and in the future "in the time to come." Such definitions do not say much at all. We cannot blame the dictionary compilers for their doodling ambiguity. The two phrases are indeed often used interchangeably without causing major confusion, like memory chipsets that fit different computer motherboards.

Then, why were our wise forebears so particular about their differences?

A scholarly discussion I came across recently shed some light on this. According to its author, the first ideogram in the Chinese expression for "in the future" (未) contains the radical implying wood or tree of dense foliage, which in old Chinese suggests shade and fruition, and by extension, palatable taste. Thus, with a bit of imagination, if not a leap of faith, one can say that the Chinese expression for "in the future" implies an uncertain, shaded prospect of fruition.

On the other hand, "in future" that contains the ideogram (将), meaning general or butcher, is far more certain. It also means, by extension, at one's command or by choice. Seeing this ideogram, I am inclined to envisioning a black cape with something unseen under its cover.

The scholar thus concluded that the Chinese expression for "in the future" implies a tomorrow beyond the scope of our vision, while "in future" a tomorrow within of our grasp. Both indicate tomorrow; the former a dangling walnut shrouded in mist, the latter a magical trunk hidden by a spell.

When we talk about a pupil with excellent grades being sure of getting into a key high school and college "in future," the phrase suggests certainty and assurance. When someone strikes it lucky in business, he or she is expected to be wealthy in future, as long as they manage their affairs properly and do not run afoul of the law. The unexpected does happen, of course. The pupil may flunk his or her next exam, freaking out because of stress, and the businessman may commit fraud, ruining their prospects. "In future" thus implies plausibility, with a hint of inevitability, within the grasp of the beholder. It carries its own momentum, as though a building project with the foundation laid, a force unleashed beyond the point-of-no-return, and a dividend forecasted; with it, calculation, convention, and business savvy.

"In the future," on the other hand, flirts with a sense of adventure and challenge. It hints at elation after groping in the dark and tireless exploration, after conquering one's own fears with wisdom and courage like a cocktail with rising bubbles of possibility.

When people harp on future being not a dream, they know there is indeed a big element of dream about future. When we pray for a future world of universal peace, we are in truth faced with flames of war and the prospect of nuclear destruction. When we talk about interstellar travel in the future, we imply mankind's epic endeavour and devotion. When we make a plethora of bold predictions about the future, we can hardly conceal our loneliness and despair at the unfathomable cosmic infinity, despite our professed courage.

"In future" has a pragmatic ring to it, while "in the future" mysterious and uncertain. The latter I much prefer. When one knows not where to get one's next meal, one thinks only of the literal tomorrow.

It is of course important to be concerned about what the future has in store. With "in future," you bide your time, as you do with hatching a fertilized egg at the required temperature, focused and putting aside other immediate problems, until the first hatchlings sing at the crack of dawn. It is like the coconuts, strewn on the beach after a storm, germinating and growing into tall palm trees given suitable soil and time, or a time bomb, hidden and ticking away until the earthshaking moment. Nothing comes from nothing. To have hope for the future is to sow a seed. You can expect a good harvest come autumn, given proper cultivation by the hand of a competent, dedicated farmer.

"In future" also has the reliability of a workflow whereby the required input produces the guaranteed output. Should there be defects, you try to find the root cause, rather than blaming the unknown. Should there be applause, do not be overjoyed. For it is merely the outcome of a certain process, as in the case of the rocket, with the entry of all necessary data, a successful launch is the norm and mid-flight explosion exception.

Thus, when we talk about "in future," we feel a sense of calm, confidence, and working according to plan. Since it is "from now on", we may still harbour trepidation and unease. But it is all a matter of time, like an image emerging on the photographic paper in the darkroom, irreversible and subject to change before halting and fixing. As things may still turn for the worse, we should never drop our guard until our ultimate success.

We should also never let trepidation prevail over hope and imagination for the future. Throughout human evolution, it is such hope and imagination that drive change. Our ancestors came down from the trees and became bipedal, not merely because of an extension of their physical prowess, but because they were inspired by their imagination. While uncertain of what lay ahead, the early humans strode on towards the receding horizon in the dim twilight, in halting steps at first, precipitating the start of a great new era.

In such light, "in future" is an antipode to "in the future" in every aspect — calm, impassioned; direct, superfluous; pragmatic, wishy-washy; orderly, wistful; gritty, far-sighted; laborious, taking it in stride; candour, shiftiness; a handy revealing tarp, the twinkling stardust beyond our reach.

The former has more to do with the individual, while the latter humanity at large.

People envision various alternatives for their future, in exquisite detail and with precision. While not denying the importance of such individualistic visions, we must also be concerned with humanity's future. When we combine the two, we are in command of a magic carpet, as it were, that will take us to the faraway, mist-shrouded canopies, of trees that bear uncertain, yet palatable fruits.

柱子的弹性

有一个故事，说的是一根柱子，一根一百年前的柱子。那根柱子很坚固，支撑着一座宏伟的大厅。那座大厅很大，大到修建的时候没有人相信一根柱子就能支撑起沉重的穹顶。年轻的建筑师用了种种科学方程式来证实他的这根柱子是何等牢靠和坚固，足够支撑。人们虽然不能反对他的公式，却可以反对由他来担当这座市政大厅的总设计师。

年轻的设计师面临一个选择。如果他坚持他的设计，他的设计就永远停留在纸上了。如果他变更他的设计，人们就看不到这根独撑穹顶的柱子了。设计师沉吟再三，修改了他的图纸，又添加了四根柱子。人们对这个更加稳妥的设计拍手叫好，据此建起了壮丽的大厦。

很多年过去了。年轻的设计师变成了墓碑，大地震袭击了城市。很多建筑都倒塌了。唯有具有五根柱子的市政大厅依然巍峨耸立。人们说，幸亏有五根柱子啊！

终于到了维修的时刻。人们惊讶地发现，除了最早设计的那根独撑大厦的柱子，其余的四根柱子距离穹顶都有一道窄窄的间隙。也就是说，它们并不承接穹顶的重量，只是美丽的摆设。

于是人们惊叹这匪夷所思的设计，给予设计者以排山倒海的赞美。回答他们的只是墓草的摇曳。

设计师没有收获生前的称誉，但他收获了一根柱子。设计师是可以怒发冲冠一走了之的，但为了他的柱子的诞生，他妥协和避让了。设计师是可以在事成之后即刻就公布他的计谋的，但为了他的柱子无可辩驳的质地，他保持了宁静的缄默。设计师是可以在一份遗嘱或一部著作中表达他的先见和果敢的，但为了他的柱子的荣誉，他不再贪恋丝毫的浮华。设计师为了他的柱子，隐没在历史的尘埃中。

这是一根有弹性的柱子。它的设计者把自己的性格赋予了它，于是柱子比设计师活得更长久。

A Resilient Column

This is a story about a weight-bearing column in a cavernous town hall built a century ago. The column was solid, supporting the vaulted roof. Before the construction of the town hall, nobody believed that a single column could hold up the weight of the roof, despite the young architect's calculations to support his design. The naysayers could not object his formulas, but had the power to revoke his appointment as the chief architect.

The young man faced a dilemma: insisting on his design which would remain on paper forever, or making modifications so that the vaulted roof would be supported by more than one column. After much deliberation, he decided to change his design and add four more columns. This won applause from all and the magnificent city hall was built.

Years had passed and the young architect departed when the town was hit by a great temblor. Many buildings collapsed, yet the town hall with its five columns stood intact. People marvelled at this and were thankful for the decision to use five columns.

However, during a later renovation, it was discovered to everyone's surprise that there was a tiny gap between the roof and the top of every column, except the one initially designed to support the vaulted roof. The four additional columns were never meant for bearing its weight.

People began to admire the incredible design, heaping praises on the young architect who did not live to receive all the accolades. The column did serve as a monument. He could have raged and stormed out when confronted with the objection, but he made a compromise for the sake of his design. He could also have made it known immediately after the town hall was completed. Yet he kept quiet so that the building was beyond reproach. He could have included an explanation in his will or left some writing about his vision and courage for posthumous publication. Yet, for the sake of the column, he refrained from any attempt at passing fame and was content to have his name banished to oblivion.

Resilient, built to last and imbued with its architect's character, the column has long survived its architect.

留一罐回忆的泡泡糖

回忆是个很奇妙的东西，如果是回忆幸福，那就好比一罐子泡泡糖；如果回忆苦闷，就是嚼了金鸡纳树皮（据说这种树皮极苦）。

负面的回忆一开始，就赶紧打住。因为每个人的内心的能量，并不像我们想象的那般强大。

不要制造剑拔弩张的险情，考验我们饱经磨砺的灵魂。我们的情绪依循着单向的险情，由俭入奢易，由奢入俭难。

我们常常会说，等待时间吧。时间可以愈合一切，但时间并不能解决所有问题。没有处理过的负面回忆就像用冰雪掩埋的尸体，一旦表面的冰雪被风暴吹走或是消融，尸体就会重新栩栩如生地显现，打我们一个措手不及。

请你有意识地将这些破碎的回忆重新拾起，将它们黏合，只看到反面的把正面也翻过来瞅一瞅，搞错了的重新恢复原状。最主要是赋予它们不同的解释和意义，你的伤口才有可能真正地愈合。而另外一些伤口，用羊肠线不能缝合，用止血钳不能锁闭，用皮肤不能覆盖，只能犹如鱼嘴般敞开着，直到墓土将它们掩埋。

但无论表面上我们如何伤痕累累，一蹶不振，破败不堪，我们依然是有价值的。这个价值与生俱来，谁也剥夺不走。除了你自己，没有任何人可以让你贬值。我们不能改变已经发生的事件，但可以改变这些事件对我们的影响。不要让过去破坏我们享受眼前美好快乐的能力。

生活中的痛苦就像盐，看你把它溶解在一个多大的容器中。如果放入一只袖珍的奶锅，完蛋了，你会被腌成酱菜。如果是海湾，那便云淡风轻了。

Memory Is a Candy Jar

Memory is miraculous. Happy memories are sweet, a jar of bubble gums, while those of sorrow bitter as the cinchona bark.

So, rein yourself in when you find yourself slipping into glum reminiscences. Your positive energy is not as strong as you believe it to be.

Don't let the negativity of sorrowful memories test your frayed nerves. For you will find it difficult to return to emotional wellbeing once you have slipped out of it.

People often say, "Let time work its magic and heal the wound." Yet, time cannot heal every wound. The raw, negative memory is the body buried in snowdrifts that will haunt us when the snow melts or is swept away in a blitz.

Gather up, examine and sort out the fragmented memories of such negativity, and put them in good order. Most importantly, give them a new interpretation, so that the old wound may truly heal. The gaping wound that simply refuses to heal, despite all possible remedies, will have to remain as it is, till death does end all.

Yet, our life, however scarred, tattered or defeated it is, has its inherent worth. We are all born with such inalienable worth. No one but you yourself can lessen it. We cannot change what has happened but can control how it will impact us. We should never let the past spoil our present enjoyment.

The bitterness of our suffering, should it be likened to a fistful of salt, varies with its concentration. If it is dissolved in a tiny cup, you end up tasting brine, whereas, in a cove, it disappears in no time.

把很深的话语，用很浅的话语说出来

有一个秘密：当你开始接受一个新的观点的时候，你以为自己已经忘记了以前习得的其他不同的说法，但那是不现实的。

不经过艰苦的放弃，以前的观念不会轻易退出，因为它们已经深入到你的脑子里了。

把很深的想法，用很浅的语言说出来，这是有能耐的表现。

让人轻松的东西，比较容易进入他人的思维系统。如果太复杂、太一本正经了，很可能从一开始就发生抗拒和逃避。再好的理念，也被隔绝，一个好的框架，只有进入了对方的大脑沟回，驻扎在那里，潜移默化地变成了行动，才算真正有效。

自我意识是人一辈子的功课，在这个过程中，充满了挑战、选择、挣扎和改变。在这个时间段中，我们将尝试我们可能达到的高度和广度，铺排我们的生命状态可以怎样绚烂多姿。

当然，你也可以选择退缩和一事无成，那样的话，你就和一个丰富的生命无缘。当你离开这个世界的时候，你会遗憾自己有那么多的想法未曾实施，大幕就已悄然闭合。

Small Words, Large Meaning

It is a little known secret: when you embrace a new idea, you don't automatically forget the old idea that you have become used to, though you may think you do.

It requires painstaking efforts to get rid of deeply ingrained ideas.

It is also no small feat to convey profound meaning in small words.

Your idea will be more readily accepted by others if it is presented in a disarming, relaxing manner. People tend to be repulsed by and shun anything too complex and pedantic, no matter how wonderful you think it is. Only when an idea is lodged in the grooves of another's cerebral cortex that dictates his or her action can it be counted as effectively communicated.

Self-knowledge requires lifelong efforts, which includes facing up to challenges, making difficult choices, soul-searching and making real change. In so doing, we explore our potentials and limitations and determine how rich and meaningful our life will be.

You can of course opt for inaction and retreat. Then you will have nothing to do with living a fulfilled life. It'll be curtains for your ideas and aspirations, leaving you to regret and lament the lost opportunities, as you walk into your twilight years.

学会欣赏心灵的成长

过去影响了现在，现在必将影响将来。只要你一息尚存，一切都还不算晚。只要你想改变，变化就会发生，只不过随着年龄的增长，变化的范围就比较狭小了，但狭小并不等于消失，永远不会有一个不能突破的界限。你可以奔突而去，决定权在你自己手中。

很喜欢一句话——死亡是成长的最后阶段。我们一生都需要成长，直到死亡。骨骼的成长，在二十几岁就已经完成了，从那以后，我们不再长高。但是，骨骼细胞还是在不断地更新当中，每一天都是新的。

你如不信，想想骨折之后，新鲜的断裂是如何卓有成效地愈合，你就会明白，即使是看起来呆若木鸡的骨头，也在日新月异地变化着，至于头发指甲这类外显的小零件，你更是可以清楚地看到它们是如何不知疲倦地增长着。

心灵呢？也一样啊，甚至成长得更快。你可以从一件事的反思上，更改几十年以来的一个错误观念。你可以在片刻的感悟中，习得一个伟大的真理。你可以从某人的一言一行中，体察到他被你忽略的丰富。你也可以一下子就识破了迷幻自己半生的谎言，从此洞若观火……

只要你学会了欣赏心灵的成长，你就会看到它电光石火般的进化，这是人生最神奇的体验之一。

Appreciate Your Spiritual Growth

What's past is prologue. As long as you live, it's never too late to start doing anything. If you resolve to change, change will happen. Even though your advancing age may whittle down its scope, the possibility of change will not wane. You can push the envelope. It all depends on your resolve.

Death is the final phase of growth — a statement that I like very much. Growth runs through our entire life until our demise. Our bone growth stops and height ceases to increase, by the time we are in our twenties. Yet new cells continuously form, replacing the old and dying; making our bones forever new.

If you have any doubt, just think how quickly a bone fracture heals. Then you will understand that even our seemingly solid old bones never cease renewing themselves, day and night. As for our hair and nails that are externally visible, it is hard not to note how untiringly they grow.

What about our mind and soul? They too are in perpetual growth and renewal, and at a more rapid pace at that. Mere introspection triggered by a certain event may overturn a misconception that you have held for decades. You see the sublime in momentary epiphany. You come to appreciate the richness of someone's character, erstwhile overlooked, in a particular act or word of theirs. In a flash, you see through the lie that has beguiled you for much of your life, becoming shrewd and incisive since.

If you learn to appreciate your spiritual growth, you will see how miraculous and momentous it is — the most amazing and life-enhancing experience one may ever have.

过去不等于未来

在美国新泽西州的一座小镇上，一个由二十六个孩子组成的班级被安排在教学楼最里面一间光线昏暗的教室里。他们中所有的人都有过不光彩的历史：有人吸过毒、有人进过管教所、有一个女孩子甚至在一年之内堕过三次胎。家长拿他们没办法，老师和学校也几乎放弃了他们。

就在这个时候，一个叫菲拉的女教师担任了这个班的辅导老师。新学年开始的第一天，菲拉没有像以前的老师那样，首先对这些孩子进行一顿训斥，给他们一个下马威，而是为大家出了一道题：

有三个候选人，他们分别是——

A．笃信巫医，有两个情妇，有多年的吸烟史，而且嗜酒如命；

B．曾经两次被赶出办公室，每天要到中午才起床，每晚都要喝大约一升的白兰地，而且曾经有过吸食鸦片的记录；

C．曾是国家的战斗英雄，一直保持素食习惯，热爱艺术，偶尔喝点酒，年轻时从未做过违法的事。

菲拉给孩子们的问题是：

如果我告诉你们，在这三个人中，有人成了众人敬仰的伟人，你们认为会是谁？猜想一下，这三个人将来各自会有什么样的命运？

对于第一个问题，毋庸置疑，孩子们都选择了C；对于第二个问题，大家的推论也几乎一致：A和B的命运肯定不妙，要么成为罪犯，要么就是需要社会照顾的废物。而C呢，一定是一个品德高尚的人，注定会成为精英。

然而，菲拉的答案却让人大吃一惊。孩子们，你们的结论也许符合一般的判断，但事实是，你们都错了。这三个人大家都很熟悉，他们是二战时期的三个著名人物——A是富兰克林·罗斯福，他身残志坚，连任四届美国总统；B是温斯顿·丘吉尔，英国历史上最著名的首相；C的名字大家也很熟悉，他叫阿道夫·

希特勒，一个夺去了几千万无辜生命的法西斯元首。学生们都呆呆地瞅着菲拉，他们简直不相信自己的耳朵。

孩子们，菲拉接着说，你们的人生才刚刚开始，以往的过错和耻辱只能代表过去，真正能代表一个人一生的，是他现在和将来的所作所为。

每个人都不是完人，连伟人也有过错。从过去的阴影里走出来吧，从现在开始，努力做自己最想做的事情，你们都将成为了不起的优秀的人才……

菲拉的这番话，改变了二十六个孩子一生的命运，如今这些孩子都已长大成人，他们中有的做了心理医生，有的做了法官，有的做了飞机驾驶员。

值得一提的是，当年班里那个个子最矮，也最爱捣乱的学生罗伯特·哈里森，后来成了华尔街上最年轻的基金经理人。

原来我们都觉得自己已经无可救药，因为所有的人都这么认为。菲拉老师第一次让我们觉醒：过去并不重要，我们还有可以把握的现在和将来。

孩子们长大后这样说。

有一位心理学家说过这样的话：你对孩子怎样

描述，他们就怎样以你描述的样子成长。你说他是个无赖，他就会慢慢变得像个无赖；你说他聪明，他就可能真的变得十分聪明。

　　许多成人不断在用自己的偏见扼杀孩子的美质，他们自己却一点儿都不知道。

Don't Let Past Cloud Your Future

In a dim room at the far back of the school building in a small town in New Jersey was a class of twenty-six students. Most of them had some undignified past — substance abuse or time in youth correctional facilities. One girl had a string of three abortions in one year. Their parents could do little and the school's faculty had all but given up on them.

Then, Fila was appointed the counsellor for the class. On the first day of the new school year, unlike her predecessors, she did not give the class a dressing-down to establish her authority. Instead, she asked the class to do a little exercise:

Deciding a) which of the following three men would

become a much-admired public personality, and b) what path each of their lives would take:

A. Someone addicted to alcohol, with a long history of smoking; a believer in witchcraft medicine, with two mistresses.

B. Someone who had been fired from his job twice, drank about a litre of brandy every evening and slept till noon, with a history of opium addiction.

C. Someone who had been a national war hero, vegetarian, art lover, occasional drinker, and never had any trouble with the law in his youth.

For question a), the students unanimously picked C; for b), they nearly all agreed that A and B were destined to become either criminals or the charge of social institutions, while C a person of noble character and a member of the social elite.

Fila's answer shocked everyone: they were all wrong, even though their conclusions were logical. The three were all well-known figures of WWII — A: Franklin Roosevelt who served four consecutive terms of the US presidency despite being paralysed from the waist down; B: Winston Churchill, the most famous Prime Minister in British history; C: Adolf Hitler, the fascist Fuehrer responsible for the deaths of millions. The students, all staring at Fila, could hardly believe their ears.

"My children," Fila rejoined, "your lives have but just begun. Whatever missteps or shame you have felt in the past represent only the past. Only the actions you take from now on will determine the life you will lead. No one can be perfect and even the greats have faltered. Walk out of the shadows of the past and strive for what you most aspire. You will all have a remarkable future that you are made for…"

Fila's words changed the course of the lives of all twenty-six students. All adults now, they count among them psychiatrists, judges, and airline pilots… It is worth mentioning that Robert

Harrison, once the most troublesome and the shortest in stature in the class, became the youngest fund manager of his time on Wall Street.

One of them later had this to say about his classmates: "We had thought ourselves worthless. So did everyone else. It was Ms. Fila who made us realize for the first time in our lives that what's past is not important and we have the now and future in our own hands."

According to one psychologist, children grow up to be what they were perceived to be. If you label a child as a good-for-nothing, he or she will likely grow up that way. If you point out that they are clever, they will eventually grow up to be smart.

Many, because of their prejudices, have stifled their children's potential to be good, without ever being aware of it themselves.

谁是你的重要他人

"重要他人"是一个心理学名词，意思是在一个人心理和人格形成的过程中，起过巨大影响甚至是决定性作用的人物。

"重要他人"可能是我们的父母长辈，或者是兄弟姐妹，也可能是我们的老师，抑或萍水相逢的路人。童年的记忆遵循着非常玄妙神秘的规律，你着意要记住的事情和人物，很可能湮没在岁月的灰烬中，但某些特定的人和事，却挥之不去，影响我们的一生。如果你不把它们寻找出来，并加以重新认识和把握，它就可能像一道符咒，在下意识的海洋中潜伏着，影响潮流和季风的走向。你的某些性格和反应模式，由于"重要他人"的影响，而被打上了深深的烙印。

这段话有点拗口，还是讲个故事吧。故事的主人公是我和我的"重要他人"。

她是我的音乐老师，那时很年轻，梳着长长的大辫子，有两个漏斗一样深的酒窝，笑起来十分清丽。当然，她生气的时候酒窝隐没，脸绷得像一块苏打饼干，木板样干燥，很是严厉。那时我大约十一岁，个子长得很高，是大队委员，也算个孩子里的小官，有很强的自尊心和虚荣心了。

学校组织"红五月"歌咏比赛，要到中心小学参赛。校长很重视，希望歌咏队能拿好名次，为校争光。最被看好的是男女小合唱，音乐老师亲任指挥。每天下午集中合唱队的同学们刻苦练习。我很荣幸被选中，每天放学后，在同学们羡慕的眼光中，走到音乐教室，引吭高歌。

有一天练歌的时候，长辫子的音乐老师突然把指挥棒一丢，一个箭步从台上跳下来，东瞄西看。大家不知所以，齐刷刷闭了嘴。她不耐烦地说，都看着我干什么？唱！该唱什么唱什么，大声唱！说完，她侧着耳朵，走到队伍里，歪着脖子听我们唱歌。大家一看老师这么重视，唱得就格外起劲。

长辫子老师铁青着脸转了一圈儿，最后走到我面前，做了一个斩钉截铁的手势，整个队伍瞬间安静下来。她叉着腰，一字一顿地说，毕淑敏，我在指挥台上总听到一个人跑调儿，不知是谁。我走下来一个人一个人地听，总算找出来了，原来就是你！一颗老鼠屎坏了一锅汤！现在，我把你除名了！

我木木地站在那里，无法接受这突如其来的打击。刚才老师在我身旁停留得格外久，我还以为她欣赏我的歌喉，唱得分外起劲，不想却被抓了个"现行"。我灰溜溜地挪出了队伍，羞愧难当地走出教室。

那时的我，基本上还算是一个没心没肺的女生，既然被罚下场，就自认倒霉吧。我一个人跑到操场，找了个篮球练起来，给自己宽心道，嘿，不要我唱歌就算了，反正我以后也不打算当女高音歌唱家。还不如练练球，出一身臭汗，自己闹个筋骨舒坦呢！（嘿！小小年纪，已经学会了中国小老百姓传统的精神胜利法）这样想着，幼稚而好胜的心也就渐渐平和下来。

三天后，我正在操场上练球，小合唱队的一个女生气喘吁吁地跑来说，毕淑敏，原来你在这里！音乐老师到处找你呢！

我奇怪地说，找我干什么？

那女生说，好像要让你重新回队里练歌呢！

我挺纳闷，不是说我走调厉害，不要我了吗？怎么老师又改变主意了？对了，一定是老师思来想去，觉得毕淑敏还可用。从操场到音乐教室那几分钟路程，我内心充满了幸福和憧憬，好像一个被发配的清官又被皇帝从边关召回来委以重任，要高呼"老师圣明"了（正是瞎翻小说，胡乱联想的年纪）。走到音乐教室，我看到的是挂着冰霜的"苏打饼干"。长辫子老师不耐烦地说，毕淑敏，你小小年纪，怎么就长了这么高的个子？！

我听出话中的谴责之意，不由自主就弓了脖子塌了腰。从此，这个姿势贯穿了我的整个少年和青年时代，总是略显驼背。老师的怒气显然还没发泄完，她说，你个子这么高，唱歌的时候得站在队列中间，你跑调儿走了，我还得让另外一个男生也下去，声部才平衡。人家招谁惹谁了？全叫你连累的，上不了场！

我深深低下了头，本来以为只是自己的事，此刻才知道还把一个无辜者拉下水，实在无地自容。长辫子老师继续数落，小合唱本来就没有几个人，队伍一下子短了半截，这还怎么唱？现找这么高个子的女生，合上大家的节奏，哪儿那么容易？现在，只剩下最后一个法子了……

老师看着我，我也抬起头，重燃希望。我猜到了老师下一步的策略，即便她再不愿意，也会收我归队。我当即下决心要把跑了的调儿扳回来，做一个合格的小合唱队员！

我眼巴巴地看着长辫子老师，队员们也围了过来。在一起练了很长时间的歌，彼此都有了感情。我这个大嗓门儿走了，那个男生也走了，音色轻弱了不少，大家也都欢迎我们归来。

长辫子老师站起来，脸绷得好似新纳好的鞋底。她说，毕淑敏，你听好，你人可以回到队伍里，但要记住，从现在开始，你只能干张嘴，绝不可以发出任何声音！说完，她还害怕我领会不到位，伸出颀长的食指，笔直地挡在我的嘴唇间。

我好半天才明白了长辫子老师的禁令——让我做一个只张嘴不出声的木头人。泪水憋在眼眶里打转，却不敢流出来。我没有勇气对长辫子老师说，如果做傀儡，我就退出小合唱队。在无言的委屈中，我默默地站到了队伍中，从此随着器乐的节奏，口形翕动，却不得发出任何声音。长辫子老师还是不放心，只要一听到不和谐音，锥子般的目光第一个就刺到我身上……

小合唱在"红五月"歌咏比赛中拿了很好的名次，只是我从此遗下再不能唱歌的毛病。毕业的时候，音乐考试是每个学生唱一支歌，但我根本发不出自己的声音。音乐老师已经换人，并不知道这段往事。她很奇怪，说，毕淑敏，我听你讲话，嗓子一点毛病也没有，怎么就不能唱歌呢？如果你坚持不唱歌，你这一门没有分数，你不能毕业。

　　我含着泪说，我知道。老师，不是我不想唱，是我真的唱不出来。老师看我着急成那样，料我不是成心捣乱，只得特地出了一张有关乐理的卷子给我，我全答对了，才算有了这门课的分数。

　　后来，我报考北京外语学院附中，口试的时候，又有一条考唱歌。我非常决绝地对主考官说，我不会唱歌。那位学究气的老先生很奇怪，问，你连《学习雷锋好榜样》也不会？那时候，全中国的人都会唱这首歌，我要是连这也不会，简直就是白痴。但我依然很肯定地对他说，我不唱。主考官说，我看你胳膊上戴着三道杠，是个学生干部。你怎么能不会唱？当时我心里想，我豁出去不考这所学校了，说什么也不唱。我说，我可以把这首歌词默写出来，如果一定要测验我，就请把纸笔找来。那老人居然真的去找纸笔了……我抱定了被淘汰出局的决心，拖延时间不肯唱歌，和那群严谨的考官们周旋争执，弄得他们束手无策。没想到发榜时，他们还是录取了我。也许是我一通胡搅蛮缠，使考官们觉得这孩子没准儿以后是个谈判的人才吧。入学之后，我迫不及待地问同学们，你们都唱歌了吗？大家都说，唱了啊，这有什么难的。我可能是那一年北外附中录取的新生中唯一没有唱歌的孩子。

在那以后几十年的岁月中，长辫子老师那竖起的食指，如同一道符咒，锁住了我的咽喉。禁令铺张蔓延，到了凡是需要用嗓子的时候，我就忐忑不安，逃避退缩。我不单再也没有唱过歌，就连当众发言演讲和出席会议做必要的发言，都会在内心深处引发剧烈的恐慌。我能躲则躲，找出种种理由推脱搪塞。会场上，眼看要轮到自己发言了，我会找借口上洗手间溜出去，招致怎样的后果和眼光，也完全顾不上了。有人以为这是我的倨傲和轻慢，甚至是失礼，只有我自己才知道，是内心深处不可言喻的恐惧和哀痛在作祟。

直到有一天，我在做"谁是你的重要他人"这个游戏时，写下了一系列对我有重要影响的人物之后，脑海中不由自主地浮现出长辫子音乐老师那有着美丽的酒窝却像铁板一样森严的面颊，一阵战栗滚过心头。于是我知道了，她是我的"重要他人"。虽然我已忘却了她的名字，虽然今天的我以一个成人的智力，已能明白她当时的用意和苦衷，但我无法抹去她在一个少年心中留下的惨痛记忆。烙红的伤痕直到数十年后依然冒着焦煳的青烟。

弗洛伊德精神分析学派认为，即使在那些被精心照料的儿童那里，也会留下心灵的创伤。因为儿童智力发展的规律，当他们幼小的时候，不能够完全明辨所有的事情，以为那都是自己的错。

孩子的成长，首先是从父母的瞳孔中确认自己的存在。他们稚弱，还没有独立认识世界的能力。如同发育时期的钙和鱼肝油会进入骨骼一样，"重要他人"的影子也会进入儿童的心理年轮。"重要他人"说过的话，做过的事，他们的喜怒哀乐和行为方式，会以一种近乎魔法的力量，种植在我们心灵最隐秘的地方，生根发芽。

在我们身上，一定会有"重要他人"的影子。

美国有一位著名的电视主持人，叫作奥普拉·温弗瑞。二〇〇三年，她登上了《福布斯》身家超过十亿美元的"富豪排行榜"，成为黑人女性获得巨大成功的代表。

父母没有结婚就生下了她，从小住的房子连水管都没有。一天，温弗瑞正躲在屋角读书，母亲从外面走进来，一把夺下她手中的书，破口大骂道："你这个没用的书呆子，把你的屁股挪到外面去！你真的以为你有什么了不起？你这个白痴！"

温弗瑞九岁就被人强暴，十四岁怀了身孕，孩子出生后就死了。温弗瑞自暴自弃，然后又暴饮暴食，吃成了一个大胖子，还曾试图自杀。那时，没有人对她抱有希望，包括她自己。就在这时，她的生父对她说：

有些人让事情发生，

有些人看着事情发生，

有些人连发生了什么都不知道。

极度空虚的温弗瑞开始挣扎奋起，她想知道自己的生命中究竟会有些什么样的事情发生。她要顽强地去做"让事情发生的人"。大学毕业之后，她获得了一个电视台主持人的位置。一九八四年，她开始主持《芝加哥早晨》的节目，大获成功，在很短的时间里成为全美收视率最高的节目。她开始发动全国范围内的读书节目，她对书狂热的爱和她的影响力，改变了很多书的命运。只要她在自己的脱口秀节目里对哪本书给予好评，那本书的销量就会节节攀升。

温弗瑞成立了自己的公司，创办了畅销杂志，还参股网络公司。她乐善好施的名声和她的节目一样响亮。她每年把自己收入的百分之十用来做慈善捐助。温弗瑞亲手推动了太多的事情发生！她认为，这主要来源于父亲的那一句话。

如果让温弗瑞写下她的"重要他人"，她的父亲一定高居榜首。他不但给予了温弗瑞生命，而且给予了她灵魂。温弗瑞的母亲也算一个。她以精神暴力践踏了幼小的温弗瑞对书籍的热爱，潜藏的愤怒在蛰伏多年之后变成了不竭的动力，使成年以后的温弗瑞，以极大的热情投入到和书籍有关的创造性劳动中，不但自己读了大量的书，还不遗余力地把好书推荐给更多的人。那个侮辱侵犯了温弗瑞的人，也要算作她的"重要他人"，这直接导致了她的巨大痛苦和放任自流，也在很多年后，主导了她执掌财富之后，把大量款项用于慈善事业，特别是援助儿童和黑人少女。

看，"重要他人"就是如此影响人的生活和命运的。

美国通用电气公司的CEO杰克·韦尔奇，被誉为全球第一CEO。在短短二十年里，韦尔奇使通用电气的市值增加了三十多倍，达到了四千五百亿美元，排名从世界第十位升到了第二位。韦尔奇说，母亲给他的最伟大的礼物就是自信心。韦尔奇从小就口吃，就是平常所说的"结巴"。在大学读书的时候，每逢星期五，天主教徒是不准吃肉的，所以在学校的餐厅里，韦尔奇经常会点一份烤面包夹金枪鱼。奇怪的是，女服务员端上来的都是两份。为什么呢？因为韦尔奇结巴，总是把这份食谱的第一个单词重复一遍，服务员就听成了"两份金枪鱼"。

面对这样一个吭吭哧哧的孩子，韦尔奇的母亲居然找出了完美的理由。她对幼小的韦尔奇说："这是因为你太聪明了，没有任何一个人的舌头，可以跟得上你这样聪明的脑袋。"

韦尔奇记住了母亲的这种说法，从未对自己的口吃有过丝毫的忧虑。他充分相信母亲的话，他的大脑比他的舌头转得更快。母亲引导着韦尔奇不断进取，直到他抵达辉煌的顶峰。母亲是韦尔奇的"重要他人"。

再讲一个苹果的故事。正确地说，是两个苹果的故事。

一位妈妈有两个孩子，她拿出两个苹果。苹果一个大一个小，妈妈让两个孩子自己来挑。大儿子很想要那个大苹果，正想着怎么说才能得到这个苹果，弟弟先开了口，说，我想要大苹果。妈妈呵斥道，你想要大的苹果，你不能说。这个大儿子灵机一动，改口说，我要这个小苹果，大苹果就给弟弟吧。妈妈说，这才是好孩子。于是，妈妈就把小苹果给了小儿子，大儿子反倒得到了又红又大的苹果。大儿子从妈妈这里得到了一条人生的经验：你心里的真心话不可以说，你要把真实掩藏起来。后来，这个大儿子就把从苹果中得到的道理应用于自己的生活，见人只说三分话，耍阴谋使诡计，巧取豪夺，直到有一天把自己送进了监狱。这个成了犯人的大儿子，如果写下自己的"重要他人"，我想他会写下妈妈和这个红苹果。

还有一位妈妈，有一篮苹果和一群孩子，也是人人都想得到大苹果。妈妈把苹果拿到手里，说，大苹果只有一个，你们兄弟这么多，给谁呢？我把门前的草坪划成三块，你们每人去修剪一块草坪。谁修剪得又快又好，谁就能得到这个大苹果。

众兄弟中的老大得到了红苹果。

他从中悟出的生活哲理是——享受要靠辛勤的劳动换取。

这个信念指导着他，直到他最后走进了白宫，成为著名的政治家。如果由他来写下自己的"重要他人"，妈妈和红苹果也会赫然在列。

看了以上的例子，你是不是对"重要他人"的重要性有了进一步的认识？也许有的人会说，我儿时的记忆早已模糊，可不记得什么他人不他人的了。我现在的所作所为，都是我自己决定的，和其他人没关系。

这个说法有一定的道理，在我们的意识中，很多决定的确是经过仔细思考才做出的。但人是感情动物，情绪常常主导着我们的决定。而情绪是怎样产生的呢？这也和我们与"重要他人"的关系密切相关。

有一位著名的心理学家，叫作艾利斯，他认为，人的非理性信念会直接影响一个人的情绪，使他遭受困扰，导致人的很多痛苦。比如，有的人绝对需要获得周围环境的认可，特别是获得每一位"重要他人"的喜爱和赞许，其实这是不可能实现的事。有人就是笃信这个观念，把它奉作真理，千辛万苦，甚至委屈自己来取悦"重要他人"，以后还会扩展到取悦更多的人，甚至所有的人，以得到其赞赏。结果呢，达不到目的不说，还令自己沮丧失望，受挫和被伤害。

传统脑神经学认为，每一种情绪都是经过大脑的分析才做出反应的，但近年来，美国的神经科学家却找到了情绪神经传输的栈道。通过精确的研究，科学家们发现，有部分原始信号是直接从人的丘脑运动中枢，引起逃避或是冲动的反应，其速度极快，大脑的分析根本来不及介入。大脑里，有一处记忆情绪经验的地方，叫作杏仁核，它将我们过去遇见事情时的情绪、反应记录下来，好像一个忠实的档案保管员。在以后的岁月中，只要一发生类似事件，杏仁核就会越过大脑的理性分析，直接做出反应。

真是"成也萧何，败也萧何"。杏仁核这支快速反应部队，既帮助我们在危急的时刻，成功地缩短应对时间，保全我们的利益，也会在某些时候形成固定的模式，贻误我们的大事。

杏仁核里储存的关于情绪应对的档案资料，不是一时一刻积存的。"重要他人"为什么会对我们产生那么重要的影响，我猜想，关于"重要他人"的记忆，是杏仁核档案馆里使用最频繁的卷宗。往事如同拍摄过的底片，储存在暗室，一有适当的药液浸泡，它们就清晰地显影，如同刚刚发生一般，历历在目，相应的对策不经大脑筛选就已经完成。

魔法可以被解除。那时你还小，你受了伤，那不是你的错。但你的伤口至今还在流血，你却要自己想办法包扎。如果它还像下水道的出口一样嗖嗖地冒着污浊的气味，还对你的今天、明天继续发挥着强烈的影响，那是因为你仍在听之任之。童年的记忆无法改写，但对一个成年人来说，却可以循着"重要他人"这条缆绳，重新梳理我们和"重要他人"的关系，重新审视我们应对问题的规则和模式。如果它是合理的，就变成金色的风帆，成为理智的一部分。如果它是晦暗的荆棘，就用成年人有力的双手把它粉碎。这个过程不是一蹴而就的，有时自己完成力不从心，或是吃力和痛苦，还需要借助专业人士的帮助，比如求助于心理咨询师。

也许有人会说，"重要他人"对我的影响是正面的，正因为心中有了他们的身影和鞭策，我才取得了今天的成绩。这个游戏，并不是要把"重要他人"像拔萝卜一样连根揪出来，然后与之决裂。对我们有正面激励作用的"重要他人"，已经成为我们精神结构的一部分。他们的期望和教诲已化成了我们的血脉，我们永远不会丢弃对他们的信任和仁爱。但我们不是活在"重要他人"的目光中，而是活在自己的努力中。无论那些经验和历史多么宝贵，对于我们来说，已是如烟往事。我们是为了自己而活着，并为自己负起全责。

经过处理的惨痛往事，已丧失实际意义上的控制魔力。长辫子老师那句"你不要发出声音"的指令，对今天的我来说，早已没有了辖制之功。

就是在最饱含爱意的环境中长大的孩子，也会存有心理的创伤。

寻找我们的"重要他人"，就是抚平这创伤的温暖之手。

当我把这一切想清楚之后，好像有热风从脚底升起，我能清楚地感受到长久以来禁锢在我咽喉处的冰霜噼噼啪啪地裂开了，一个轻松畅快的我，从符咒下解放了出来。从那一天开始，我可以唱歌了，也可以面对众人讲话而不胆战心惊了。从那一天开始，我宽恕了我的长辫子老师，并把这段经历讲给其他老师听，希望他们面对孩子稚弱的心灵，懂得该是怎样地谨慎小心。童年时留下烙印的负面情感，难以简单地用时间的橡皮轻易地擦去。这就是心理治疗的必要性所在。和谐的人格不是从天上掉下来的，而是和深刻的内省有关。

告诉缺水的人哪里有水源，告诉寒冷的人哪里有篝火，告诉生病的人哪里有药草，告诉饥饿的人哪里有野果，这些都是天下最好的礼物。

如果让我选出自己最喜欢的游戏，我很可能要把票投给"谁是你的重要他人"。感谢这个游戏，它在某种程度上修改了我的人生。人的创造和毁灭都是由自己完成的，人永远是自己的主人。即使当他在最虚弱、最孤独的时候，他也是自己的主人。当他开始反省自己的状况，开始辛勤地寻找自己的生命所依据的法则时，他就渐渐变得平静而快乐了。

Your Significant Other

In psychology, a "significant other" is any person who has a strong influence on, or plays a decisive role in, one's life.

"The significant other" can be one's parent, a family elder, sibling, teacher or even someone met by chance. Childhood memory has its own mysterious logic. Some people or events are easily forgotten and lost in the mist of the bygone, no matter how hard we try to recall them, while others have a persistent influence on our life, however we try to banish them from our mind. We need to identify and re-examine our "significant others," for they may continue to cast a spell, sometimes not altogether positive, on our character and emotional responses, like ocean currents fuelling storms and trade winds.

This may all sound a bit baffling and wordy. So let me share with you a story; one about me and a "significant other."

She was my school music teacher, young at the time. She wore a long braid. Two deep dimples, like little dents in cream, would show when she smiled sweetly, and be gone when she was angry. Then her face would be wooden and stern. I was eleven then; gangly, vain and with a big ego. I was something of a student leader, a committee chair of the Young Pioneers Battalion.

In May that year, choral competitions were held in the school district to celebrate historical anniversaries throughout the month. The headmaster was keen to see the choral society winning top prizes, to bring glory to the school. Its mixed chorus was most favoured to win. The music teacher took up the role of the conductor. Being luckily picked to be a member of the chorus, I would go to the music room for rehearsals each afternoon after classes were over, being the envy of all my classmates.

One day in the middle of a rehearsal, the music teacher suddenly flung her baton and bolted down the podium, which stunned us into silence, not knowing what to do next. She snapped, "Why do you all stare at me? Carry on! Sing!" Saying which, she pricked her ears and paced up and down the rows, with her head tilting to the side, listening intently. Encouraged, we broke into a more vigorous bout of singing.

The stern-faced music teacher went around the group before stopping in front of me. With a quick sweep of her hand in the air, she brought the chorus to an abrupt stop. Her hands on her hips, she spat out her words one by one, "One of you was out of tune. I came down and listened to each of you. Now I know: it is you, Bi Shumin, a bad apple spoiling the lot. You are dismissed, now!"

I was dumbstruck by this out-of-the-blue

blow. It was hard to swallow. I had thought the music teacher's lingering beside me a sign of appreciation, at which I had sung with even greater gusto, only to be caught by her red-handed. I walked off with tail between legs, crushed by a sense of shame.

I was by and large rather unimpressionable, straight to a fault. I was penalized and kicked out of the chorus. So be it. I went to the outdoor basketball court, picked up a ball and started practicing by myself. I said to myself: "Hey, it is not the end of the world. I never wanted to be a soprano singer anyway. Why don't I just play some ball and sweat it out? It will make me feel good all over again." The mere thought of it soothed me, quelling whatever childish wrath and combativeness I had left. (Young as I was, I had learned the trick of self-deception, so-called "moral victory," long practiced by humble nobodies).

Three days later when I was dribbling a ball on the basketball court, a girl from the chorus ran up to me, huffing and puffing, and said, "So you are here, Bi Shumin. The music teacher has been looking for you everywhere!"

"What for?" said I, finding it odd.

"It seems she wants you back in the chorus."

I was befuddled. Didn't she just get rid of me for singing out of tune? What made her change her mind? Perhaps she thought I might still be good for the chorus after she had thought it over? My heart began to be filled with hope in the short walk from the ball court to the music room, like the exiled mandarin about to be pardoned by the emperor. Perhaps I should be prepared for an invocation of gratitude for the sudden change of fortune. However, as I stepped into the music room, I was met by the same stern countenance and the pithy words, "Bi Shumin, why are you so tall for your age?"

Sensing her acerbic tone, my shoulders slumped and my head hung low involuntarily, which had since become my signature posture through adolescence and youth. The teacher seemed to have yet to recover from her wrath. She fumed, "You are so tall and had to be placed in the middle of the row. After I asked you to leave the chorus, thanks to your singing out of tune, I had to remove the boy next to you, too, to balance the section. It's all your fault that he had to go."

My head hung even lower. I felt ashamed of bringing down an innocent fellow chorus member with me, while the culprit should have been I alone. The teacher continued, "It was a small chorus to start with. With the two of you being removed, how are we going to perform? It's almost impossible to find someone as tall as you who can also sing as well as others in the chorus. Here is what I'll do ... "

With her eyes fixed on me, I looked up, hope rising again. She was returning me to the fold, however reluctant, I thought. I decided right then that I would be good and sing in tune with others.

As I looked at the teacher pleadingly, my fellow chorus members hemmed in. There was camaraderie among us, for we had rehearsed together for some time and grown close. The chorus's singing was made lesser by the departure of me, with my boisterous voice, and the boy. So they would be happy to see us back.

The music teacher rose to her feet, her face solemn and stern, saying, "Listen, Bi Shumin. You can come back to the chorus. But remember, you are going to mime singing only, without ever making any sound." Saying which, she raised her long and bony index finger and planted it right in front of my lips for good measure.

It took me a moment to get her point — I was only to mime singing like a puppet and forbidden to utter any sound. Tears welled up and I tried to hold them back. I did not dare to say to the teacher wearing a long braid that I would rather not be in the chorus than sing without using my voice. Repressing my sense of injustice, I rejoined the group and began mouthing the lyrics to the music. The teacher was still suspicious and would shoot a piercing glance my way, every time she suspected an incongruous note.

We eventually won a decent prize at the choral competition. However, I became tongue-tied whenever I was to sing. For the music subject in our graduation exam, we were each required to sing a song. I simply could not bring myself to sing with my voice. By then we had a new music teacher who knew nothing about what had happened. Puzzled, she asked, "I see you have no problem with speech. Why can't you sing? If you keep refusing to sing, you won't get a passing grade in this subject and won't be allowed to graduate."

Teary-eyed, I told her, "It's not that I choose not to sing, miss. I am simply unable to sing." Seeing me flustered and knowing that I wasn't trying to make things difficult for her, she agreed to let me do a written test instead, with questions she wrote specifically for me. I got a full score, which allowed me to pass the exam and graduate.

When I applied to the Affiliated High School of Beijing Foreign Studies University, I was again asked to sing at the interview. I told the interviewer flatly that I could not sing. The interviewer, with a bookish look about him, was rather startled, "You can't even sing something as simple as 'Learn from Lei Feng'?" I said firmly, "No!" though it must have made me look rather dumb because it was virtually a national song.

The interviewer pursued, "You must be a Young Pioneer leader since you are wearing the three-stripe badge. How can you not be able to sing this song?"

"If you insist, give me a pen and a sheet of paper and I will write down the lyrics for you," said I, by then ready to quit if I was forced to sing.

The elderly interviewer went for a pen and paper... I tried as much as I could to dodge singing, dragging my feet and being prepared even to withdraw from applying. In the end, the exacting recruiters threw up their hands. When the names of admitted applicants were published, I saw my name on the list. Perhaps the haggling and holding my ground had convinced them that I might make a good negotiator. When the school term started, I asked my classmates if they had all sung in their interviews. They all did and it was no big deal, so they told me. I was perhaps the only recruit that year that had refused to sing.

In the decades that followed, the upturned index finger of my music teacher put a damper on my singing voice like a spell. What's more, it had made me cringe whenever a public speech was in order. I stopped singing altogether and would panic every time I was to speak at meetings or conferences. I avoided such occasions like the plague, using all kinds of excuses. I would slip out to use the washroom when it was about to be my turn, ignoring others' looks or any possible consequences. Some hinted that this was a sign of my arrogance and disrespect for others. I knew too well it was the unspeakable fear and pain that had haunted me like a ghost.

It was not until one day I jogged down a list of persons

that had had important influences on me, in the exercise of "Naming Your Significant Others," did I realize that the music teacher was one such person. The thought of the steely, stern look on her face would send chills down my spine; a face that otherwise would have shown two beautiful dimples. My painful memory of her was indelible, though I had all but forgotten her name. With the acquired wisdom of a grownup, I could understand her banal intention and predicament. Yet, the searing pain was as raw as ever, even decades later.

According to Freud's psychoanalytic theory, even children who are well cared for may suffer various types of trauma in childhood. With limited rational capacity, they cannot fully comprehend all the unresolved conflicts in certain phases of childhood, which give rise to a sense of guilt.

As children grow up, they begin to see themselves through the eyes of their parents, being weak and unable to understand the world on their own. As supplements of calcium and cod liver oil taken during the growth spurt in adolescence end up in our bones, "significant others" cast long shadows on a child's personality. Their words, actions, emotions and behaviour take on near-magic power, taking root in the most obscure crevices of a child's mind. In each of us, there are shadows cast by our "significant others."

Oprah Winfrey is a well-known talk show host in the US who made the Forbes's "rich list" in 2003 with a personal net worth of over one billion dollars. She is deemed one of the most successful African American women. Yet, she was born to unmarried parents and in childhood lived in a house without plumbing. One day, Winfrey was reading in the corner of the room when her mother barged in and snatched her book from her, yelling, "Move your ass out of here, you useless bookworm. You think you'll ever come to much? What an idiot!"

She was sexually abused when she was nine. She was pregnant when she was fourteen and gave birth to a child who soon died. She was desperate, giving up all hope, and had a string of problems with compulsive eating. She became overweight and at one time suicidal. At the time, no one had any faith in her doing any good, not even she herself. Then, her biological father said to her: some people make things happen; others look on as things happen; still others don't even know what has happened to them.

Grappling with her sense of despair, she decided to find out what life might offer and to strive to make things happen. After college, she got a job as a news anchor at a local TV station. In 1984, she began hosting the morning talk show, AM Chicago. The show became hugely successful and, in time, the highest-rated talk show in America. She also launched the Oprah's Book Club, spawning interest in book-reading. Energized by her passion for reading, the book discussion segment became so influential that any title she promoted became an overnight best-seller.

She then started her own company, launched a popular magazine, and invested in internet companies. She is well-known for her generous giving, donating one-tenth of her income to philanthropy. She made many things happen and it was all because of the words of her father, so she said.

If she were to be asked for her list of the "significant others," her father's name would be right there at the top. He is both her biological and her spiritual father. Winfrey's mother would also make the list. For the anger triggered by her trampling of young Winfrey's love for books became the force that drove her passion for reading and creative work. Not only did she read most extensively, but she also spared no effort in recommending good books to others. The man that molested her would probably be another "significant other." He inflicted tremendous pain on her and made her almost give up on herself. It probably also motivated her, after she became rich, to donate large sums of money to philanthropy, and in particular, to helping children and young African American girls.

Such is the power of the significant other on a person's life and destiny.

Jack Welch, the former CEO of General Electric Company was once named the world's No. 1 CEO. In just two decades of his tenure at GE, the company's value increased by more than thirtyfold, reaching U$450 billion. It became the second highest ranked company in the world, moving up from the previous tenth place. Welch once said that perhaps the single greatest gift his mother gave him was self-confidence. He grew up with a speech impediment, a stammer that wouldn't go away, which could sometimes be rather comical. In college, he often ordered a tuna fish on white toast on Fridays when Catholics in those days couldn't eat meat. Inevitably, the waitress would return with not one but a pair of sandwiches, having heard his order as "tu-tuna sandwiches." For his son's stuttering, his mother served up the perfect excuse. "It's because you're so smart," she would say to the young Welch. "No one's tongue could keep up with a brain like yours."

He took that to heart and for years never worried about his stammer. He totally believed what she told him: that his mind worked faster than his mouth. She gave him unyielding admonitions and urged him to go for it until he reached the apex of his career. His mother is his "significant other."

Now I will share with you a story about an apple, or two apples, to be precise — one large and the other small. Two siblings were asked by their mother to each pick one. The older wanted to have the large apple but struggled for a way of saying it, before his younger brother blurted, "I want the large apple." The mother told him off: "Even if you want to get the large apple for yourself, you don't say it like that." Hearing which, the older son said, "I will have the small apple. Give the large one to my brother." "There is the good boy," said the mother. She went on to give the large, succulent apple to the older son and the small one to his brother. The older son learned a lesson: Don't always speak your mind; covering up the truth when the occasion demands. He was to apply this to all his pursuits in life, evasive, scheming and taking advantage of others always, until one day he found himself in prison. If he were to make a list of the most influential people in his life, it would likely include his mother with that large red apple.

Another story about apples: a mother with a bushel of apples and three sons who all wanted the largest apple. Holding the largest apple in her hand, the mother declared that it would be a prize for the one who finished the task, divided equally among them, of mowing the lawn in front of the house first and best.

The eldest son eventually got the largest apple. He also learned his lesson: no pains, no gains. With this lesson guiding him, he ended up winning the White House race and becoming a remarkable statesman. If he were to put down his list of "significant others," his mother with the red apple would feature prominently.

Did these anecdotes shed light on how important "significant others" can be? Some may say that their childhood memory has become hazy, that they can't think of any others in their early life, significant or otherwise, and that whatever they do today is their own decision and has nothing to do with others.

There is some truth to their claim. Indeed we often deliberate and make decisions before we act. Yet humans, being the species capable of emotions, can also be influenced by their moods in decision-making. And the way our emotions rise is also closely related to and affected by our "significant others."

The renowned psychologist Alice Miller suggested that an individual's irrational beliefs may impact his moods, making him confused and miserable. For example, he may be convinced that he must try hard to please all those around him and won the affection and approval of all and, in particular, of his "significant others," to the detriment of himself. In the end, not only is that impossible, but it will also cause him to suffer setbacks, disappointment and harm.

According to classical neurology, each emotion is a response to external stimuli being processed by the brain. However, American neuroscientists, in exploring new pathways by which emotions are triggered, have discovered after rigorous research that the "fight and flight" response can be caused directly by signals from the thalamus and the motor centre of the brain. The amygdalae, two almond-shaped clusters of nuclei deep in our brain, are responsible for memory and emotional responses, with a role akin to that of an archivist. They are capable of directly inducing responses, bypassing rational processing by the brain.

The almond-shaped amygdalae, a rapid response centre as it were, cut down our response time and save us in moments of peril. But they can also wreak havoc with the conditioned responses;

like an "imperial counsel being capable of both making and breaking the chance of military success," as the saying goes.

Emotional responses are stored over time in the amygdalae. Our memories of the "significant others" are the most frequently accessed in the amygdalae archive, hence their tremendous influence on our life. Memories of events and people are like latent images on exposed photographic films. They are revealed given the right chemical solutions, as stimuli eliciting emotional responses like a spell.

But the spell can be broken. The reason that a childhood trauma still haunts you, affecting your life now and in the future, is that you let it do so. The gaping old wounds may refuse to heal and the bygone continues to give, as it were, the obnoxious smell. No one can change their childhood memory, but as a grownup, you can examine the influences of your "significant others" and your responses. If your responses are rational, let them be part of your constitution, your rational mind. If they are dark and glum, like thorny thistles, then uproot and crush them. Yet, this will be a gradual process and one may need professional help, such as that of a counselling psychologist if it becomes too painful and overwhelming.

For some, the influences of their "significant others" may have been all positive. They owe their success to the inspiring examples and encouragement of their "significant others." The point of the exercise is not to dislodge all our significant others and make a clean break from their influences. Their positive influences become part of our psyche, and their teachings and expectations are in our blood. Our faith in and affection for them will not wane. But we will not live in their shadow. We will strive to live the life we aspire to live. What we have experienced in the past becomes bygone, however precious the memory. We will all live, and be wholly responsible for, our own lives.

Any traumatic experience from the past loses its power to haunt us after our examination and processing. The curse by my music teacher with the long braid — "You should not make any sound" — has long ceased to hold any sway over me.

Even children growing up in the most loving family may have suffered psychological trauma. Identifying and examining our "significant others" is an exercise to mitigate any effects of such trauma.

As I thought about all this, I felt a warm glow, sensing the lifting and unravelling of the iciness in my throat and feeling liberated from the sinister spell. I could again sing and speak in front of an audience without fear. I have also since forgiven my music teacher with the long braid. I have told the story to others in the teaching profession, in hopes of their being tactful when talking to young children with frail sensitivity. Negative experiences etched in a child's memory are hard to erase by the hand of time. This is when psychological counselling may come in useful. Profound introspection underscores a balanced personality that does not come naturally.

Tell people where to find what they need — the spring

for those in need of water; the campfire for those shivering from cold; the bush for the famished where wild fruits and berries abound. They are the best gifts to them in the world.

If I were to choose my favourite exercise, I would very likely pick "Name Your Significant Others." I am grateful for having had the chance to do it, which to some extent changed my life. We are each responsible for our own success and demise. We are the master of our own destiny, even in our weakest or loneliest moments. When we start to reflect upon the state of our existence and seek enlightenment as to the rules by which to live our lives, we find ourselves becoming joyful and tranquil.

指纹状的菌落

那时我是一个年轻的实习医生。在外科做手术的时候，最害怕的是当一切消毒都已完成，正准备戴上手套，穿上洁白的手术衣，开始在病人身上动刀操练的时候，突然从你的身后，递过来一只透明的培养皿。护士长不苟言笑地指示道，你留个培养吧。这是一句医学术语，翻成大众的语言就是用你已经消完毒的手指，在培养基上抹一下。然后护士长把密闭的培养皿送到检验科，在暖箱里孵化培养。待到若干时日之后，打开培养皿，观察有无菌落生长，以检查你在给病人手术前，是否彻底消毒了你的手指。如果你的手不干净，就会在手术时把细菌带进腹腔、胸腔或是颅脑，引起感染。严重时会危及病人的生命。

我很讨厌这种抽查。要是万一查出你手指带菌，多没面子！于是我消毒的时候就格外认真。外科医生的刷手过程，真应了一句西谚：在碱水里洗三次。先要用硬毛刷子蘸着肥皂水，一丝不苟地直刷到腋下，直到皮肤红到发痛，再用清水反复冲洗，恨不能把你的胳膊收拾得像一根搓掉了皮、马上准备凉拌的生藕。然后整个双臂浸泡在百分之七十五的酒精桶里，度过难熬的五分钟。最烦人的是胳膊从酒精桶里拔出后，为了保持消过毒的无菌状态，不能用任何布巾或是纸张擦拭湿淋淋的皮肤，只有在空气中等待它们渐渐晾干。平日我们打针的时候，只涂一小坨酒精，皮肤就感到辛凉无比。因为酒精在挥发的时候，带走了体内的热能，是一种强大的物理降温过程。现在我们的上肢大面积裸露着，假若是冬天，不一会儿就冻得牙齿鼓点一般叩个不停。

更严格的是在所有过程中，双臂都要像受刑一般高举着，无论多么累，都不能垂下手腕，更严禁用手指接触任何异物。简言之，从消毒过程一开始，你的手就不是你的手了，它成了一件有独立使命的无菌工具。

我的同学是一位漂亮女孩，她的手很美，鸡蛋清一般柔嫩，但在猪毛刷子日复一日的残酷抚摸下，很快变得粗糙无光。由于酒精强烈的脱脂作用，手臂也像枯树干，失去了少女特有的润泽。单看上肢，我都像一个老太婆了。她愤愤地说。

以后的日子里，她洗手的时候开始偷工减料。比如该刷三遍，她一遍就草草过关。只要没人看见，她就把白皙的胳膊从酒精桶里解放出来，独自欣赏……有一天，我们正高擎双手，像俘虏兵投降一样傻站着，等着自己的臂膀风干时，她突然说，我的耳朵后边有点痒。

这是一件小事，但对于此时的我们来说，却是一件很难办的事。消过毒的手已被管制，我俩就像卸去双臂的木偶，无法接触自己的皮肤。按照惯例，只有呼唤护士，烦她代为搔痒。因手术尚未开始，护士还在别处忙，眼前一时无人。同学说痒得不行，忍不了。我说，要不咱们俩像山羊似的，脑袋抵着脑袋，互相蹭蹭？她说，我又不是额头痒，是脖子下面的凹处，哪里抵得着？我只好说，你就多想想邱少云吧。同学美丽的面孔在大口罩后面难受得扭歪了。突然，可能痒痛难熬，她电光石火地用消过毒的手，在自己耳朵后面抓了一把。

我惊愕得说不出话来，几乎不相信自己的眼睛。正在这时，护士长走了进来，向我和同学伸出了两个细菌培养皿……

　　其实事情在这个份儿上，还是可以挽救的。同学可以直率地向护士长申明情况，说自己的手已经污染，不能接受检验。然后再重复烦琐的洗手过程，她依旧可以正常参加手术。但她什么也没有说，哆哆嗦嗦地探出手指，在培养基上捻了一下……那天是一个开腹手术，整个过程我都恍惚不安，好像自己参与了某种阴谋。

　　病人术后并发了严重的感染，刀口溃烂腐败，高烧不止，医护人员陷入紧张的治疗和抢救。经过化验，致病菌强大而独特。它是从哪里来的呢？老医生不止一次面对病历自言自语。过了几天，手术者的细菌培养结果出来了，我的同学抹过的培养基上，呈现出茂密的细菌丛，留下指纹状的菌落阴影，正是引致病人感染的险恶品种。

　　那一刻，我的同学落下一串串眼泪。由于她的过失，病人承受了无妄之灾。她的手在搔痒的时候，沾染了病菌，又在手术过程中污染了腹腔，酿成他人巨大的痛苦。

　　病人的命总算挽救回来了，但这件事被我牢牢地记在心里，不敢忘怀。

　　随着年岁渐长，我从中悟出了许多年轻时忽略的道理。

首先是感染和腐败几乎是一种必然。牛奶放在那里，不加温不冷冻，随它去，就一定会变酸发臭。没有特殊的防腐措施，想在常温下保持牛奶的新鲜品质，是痴人说梦。铁会生锈，木头会腐烂，水面布满青苔，密闭的房屋长毛生霉，空气发出臭鸡蛋的味道……腐败几乎是无处不在，见缝下蛆。我那个同学只用手搔了一下耳后，千真万确，仅此一下，病菌潜伏到了她的手上，播种到手术刀口里，就引发了恶劣后果。细菌的生命力和感染力，真是不可思议的强大，任何侥幸心理都是万万要不得的。

二是防感染和腐败的措施，只要认真执行，是一定有效的。凡是认真执行了刷手要诀的人，每次细菌培养就都是阴性，他们的手术后感染率几乎是零。感染和腐败不是不可战胜的，只要有了切实可行、行之有效的措施，严格地执行用鲜血换来的经验教训，腐败和感染可以被制伏。

三是同样的致病菌，每个人的抵抗力不同，结局也就有天壤之别。潜伏在同学耳朵旁的细菌，肯定已在她身上生存多时，相安无事。可是移植到了病人身上，就引发了骇人的后果，盖因彼此的素质不同，结果也就因人而异。同学是正常人，有良好的防御系统，所以病菌伤害不了她。但开刀的病人就不同了，自身抵抗力薄弱，雪上加霜，差点要了性命。当然我这样说，并不是要求病榻上的人要有运动健将一般的体魄，只是说加强自身的防御系统，是抵御病菌最有效的武器。一个人遭受细菌的感染不可避免，但有了足够的准备，即使敌人侵入，也可以在最短的时间内将其歼灭。

最后是要找到一个黄金般的点。应该说抗感染的杀菌药物是十分有效的，医生把致病的细菌培养出来，它就成了靶子。把各种抗菌药物，以不同的浓度加到培养皿里，观察哪种药物杀菌最有效，然后对症下药，把病菌用最敏感的药物压下去，力争在最短的时间里，取得胜利。记得老医生总是很仔细地计算用药的剂量，根据病情，反复测算。我看得不耐烦，说搞这么复杂干什么，不是治病救人吗，当然剂量越大效果越好。老医生说，任何药物都是有毒性的，正是为了治病救人，才要找到一个最恰当的剂量，既干净彻底地消灭了病菌，又最大限度地保护挽救病人，这是一门艺术。一个好医生的职责，就是要找到这个像黄金分割率一般宝贵的结合点……

我记住了他的话，但更深刻地领悟它，却是在年岁渐长，看到了许多医学领域以外的问题之后。

病菌和微生物向我们撒下天罗地网，由它们引致的感染与腐败，每日每时都在发生。和形形色色的腐败菌做斗争，也许将贯穿经济和政治生活的整个历史。我们将会有更优秀的医生，我们将会有更强大的药品，我们将会有更严格的消毒手段，但加强自身的抵抗力，永远是最重要的。在旷日持久的战斗中，不断地完善自己、修复自己，人类才会保持蓬勃的生命力，欣欣向荣。

Bacterial Colony in a Fingerprint Pattern

I was a young hospital intern then. One protocol before each surgery that I always feared was: a Petri dish thrust before me from behind by the head nurse, after I had finished scrubbing my hands and was about to put on the white scrubs. "Time to collect a sample for the culture plate," she would announce matter-of-factly. In layman's terms, I was to swipe the surface of the agar with my index finger. The agar plates would then be sealed, sent to the lab and kept at the required temperature for several days. Then they would be read for any sign of bacterial growth to determine the efficacy of antisepsis. If a surgeon's hands were not properly scrubbed, infections in the surgery sites such as the abdomen, chest or brain could cause death in the most extreme cases.

I hated such sampling. I hated being put on the spot, should they find that my hands had not been properly scrubbed. Thus I took hand scrubbing very seriously, which traditionally was done in a chlorinated lime solution three times before surgery. I would start with soap and brush, vigorously scrubbing my hands and arms to a few inches above the elbow until the skin turned red with pain, and then rinsing them under running water. Then, I would raise my scrubbed hands above elbows, keeping them from touching anything, as though they were ready-to-eat turnips, before plunging them in a container of 75% alcohol solution for an agonizing five-minute. Then the most annoying part: having my hands and arms air dried after the alcohol emersion. No towel or tissue, to avoid contamination. You feel cold in the tiny patch of skin when it is prepared with alcohol swabs before injection. For alcohol takes heat away as it evaporates. Now, with both arms exposed after being dipped in alcohol, I was soon so cold that my teeth would chatter like the clinking castanets.

What's more, my hands had to remain above my elbows all the time, as if under some sort of torture. I was not to touch any surface with my fingers. In short, once the scrubbing is done, my hands, disinfected and ready for their mission, no longer felt mine.

A fellow intern was a young woman with good looks, and her soft hands delicate as hard-boiled egg white. However, after repeated scrubbing with a pig-hair brush, they turned coarse. With the deep cleansing by alcohol, her arms lost the lustre of a young woman's skin, wrinkled like the bark of a dying tree. "I am an old woman by the look of the skin of my arms," said she, vexed.

So, she began to cut corners. She would scrub her hands with the brush only once, instead of three times. As long as no one was watching, she would pull her fair-skinned arms from the alcohol solution, admiring them daintily. One day as both of us stood with our arms raised for drying, like two captives with their hands raised in submission, she blurted, "I felt itchy behind my ear."

A trivial matter under normal circumstances, it was a tough challenge then. With our hands all disinfected and held up as required like stiff marionettes, we were unable to touch any part of our skins. Usually, she could have to ask a nurse to give her a scratch. As the operation was yet to start, the nurses were all busying themselves elsewhere, with none being around. My fellow intern groaned, saying the itch was unbearable.

"You could rub your head against mine," I offered, "like mountain sheep butting heads."

"That won't do. The itch is behind my ear, not in my forehead," said she.

"Then, try think about the martyr Qiu

Shaoyun who didn't move for the protection of others when trapped in an incendiary bomb fire."

Her pretty face behind the surgical mask twitched out of intense itchiness behind her ear. Caving in, she gave it a quick scratch with one of her disinfected hands.

Flabbergasted, I could hardly believe my eyes. Just at that moment, the head nurse came over and thrust two Petri dishes right in front of us.

Even at this stage, a tragedy could have been averted. She could have admitted to the head nurse that her hand had been contaminated and she needed another scrubbing before taking part in the surgery. However, she said nothing, holding out a finger gingerly and swiping the surface of the agar with it, while I stood by, stunned and ill at ease, feeling like an accomplice in some sinister ploy.

It was an abdominal surgery. The patient suffered severe postoperative infection, running a persistent fever, with the incision wound refusing to heal, and pus, abscess draining from it. The patient had to be placed under intensive care.

The lab test found a unique and powerful strain of bacteria. "Where could they come from?" the senior surgeon mumbled to himself over and again. A few days later, when the results of culture plates came back, that of my fellow intern showed a colony of bacteria in a dark, fingerprint pattern. They were of the strain that had caused the patient's infection.

Tears trickled down her cheeks, as she realized that her breach of protocol had led to the surgical wound infection. When she scratched behind her ear, her hand was contaminated, which resulted in the undue tragedy and the patient's tremendous suffering.

The patient's life was eventually saved. Yet the incident was etched in my memory; a lesson I had never forgotten. As I grew older, I came to see several points that I had missed earlier when I was young.

First of all, contamination and deterioration

are inevitable if not effectively prevented. Milk, for example, will turn sour and smell foul, if it is not heated or left unrefrigerated. It is idiotic to think milk, without special treatment, will remain fresh when left out in room temperature. Iron will rust and wood rot; water becomes brackish and stuffy room musty. Even air can smell like rotten eggs. Degeneration is ubiquitous and bacteria omnipresent. My fellow intern only scratched the itch behind her ear once and the bacteria were transported by her hand to the incision site, resulting in a serious infection. The power of the bacteria is incredibly strong and nothing should be left to chance when antisepsis is concerned.

Second, never fiddle with antisepsis protocols. Properly followed, they deliver effective results. All who abide by the hand scrubbing protocol will see their culture plates come back negative. The rate of postoperative infections for their surgeries can be next to zero. Infection and deterioration are preventable, with effective measures developed following dire consequences of poor disinfection.

Third, people's resistance to the same pathogen may vary, resulting in vastly different outcomes. The bacteria behind my fellow intern's ear that were no threat to her wellbeing was life threatening when transplanted to the patient's surgery site. It all comes down to their physiological conditions. The former with her body's self-defence intact could stand the bacterial attack, whereas the latter with weakened self-defence after surgery nearly died of infection. Not suggesting that a bedridden patient should have athletic robustness, I do want to stress that enhancing one's body's self-defence is most effective in fighting infections. One can never be free from the risk of infection, but better self-defence will help ensure more effective treatment and faster recovery.

Last, it is important to determine the right dosage for antibiotics. They are usually effective in treating bacterial infections. Doctors test antibiotics of varying dosages on bacterial colonies in Petri dishes to determine which is most effective. I remember a senior physician testing repeatedly to determine the right dosage for each course of medication he prescribed. I would grow impatient, asking why he should be so fastidious since greater dosages should naturally have better results. "All medicines have a level of toxicity," he would reply. "It is important to prescribe the right dosage for each patient, delivering the most effective cure while minimizing side effects. Getting it right is an art. Every good physician has to strike the right balance, to find the golden ratio…"

I remembered his words, but their profound meaning struck home with me only after I had had my share of trials and challenges beyond medicine.

Pathogens and microorganisms are everywhere, never ceasing to cause infection and degeneration, just as risks of corruption are ever present in the world of business and politics. We will have more and better physicians, more effective medicines and more stringent antiseptic protocols. Yet, all this should not lessen the efforts to enhance the body's self-defence. In the perennial battle against infection, we should continuously enhance and remedy such self-defence, so that humanity can be assured of a thriving future.

好心态

　　一个健全的心态，比一百种智慧都更有力量。

　　现在把智商炒得火热，可是我总觉得很多事情没办好，不是我们的智商不够，而是心态不稳。心理现在也成了一个几乎被说滥了的词。棋下输了，会说，其实是在心理上输了。跳水砸了，会说不是技不如人，而是心理上的问题。考试慌张，没能考出应有的成绩，自然也是心理上的毛病了……凡此种种，还可以举出很多。有时心想，心理问题变成了一个大箩筐，什么东西都可以丢进去。

　　不过，心理还真是一个大箩筐，也许它的容积，比我们想象的更大。我们的大脑，虽说是整个机体的总司令，但其实只占了整个身体能量的一小部分。还有一大部分，是习惯成自然，类乎山高皇帝远的封建诸侯国，自成体系。也就是说，机体几乎是在独立自主的情形下，下意识地完成很多重要工作。比如，正常时分，你能知道自己的胃肠道是如何消化食物的吗？能知道自己的血压是如何调整的吗？想必大多数人一脸茫然。

如果人们紧张慌乱手足无措，诸侯小国也顿时进入了非常状态。放弃了平日的稳定和协调，乱成一锅粥，其后果不堪设想。这就是为何在比赛中，有的选手会因为过度紧张，犯一些不可思议的低级错误。

说到底，也没什么不可思议的。紧张几乎是万恶之源，一旦机体进入了不协调状态，我们会词不达意、手足无措、丢三落四、张口结舌、漏洞百出、匪夷所思……总之，各种谬误风起云涌，让人防不胜防。

有人看到这里，就会很悲观，说照你这样一讲，岂不就没救了？无论我们事先准备得如何好，到时候，神通广大的潜意识一作乱，我们就前功尽弃、毁于一旦了啊！的确是这样。平日锻炼自己养成健全的心态，遇事冷静不慌，全部身心高度协调，这比智慧更重要。

Mental Equilibrium

A balanced mind and a positive mindset are a hundredfold more powerful than mere smartness.

Despite all the current hoopla about IQ, I have always felt that it is the lack of mind's equanimity, rather than wits, that has prevented us from achieving many a desired outcome. The word "psychological" is so overused that you see it applied everywhere. When someone lost a chess game, the defeat would be described as psychological. A diver who lost his bid for a championship title would have been disadvantaged by his psychological deficiency more than technical flops. Failing to achieve expected scores at exams was blamed on psychological issues.... One wonders if such an all-encompassing term could perhaps merit the name of any problem.

Yet our mind does have extensive power, much more encompassing than we may have imagined. The brain, the "commander-in-chief" of our body, only consciously controls a small portion of its activities. A much larger portion of bodily functions work as though by force of habit and autonomously, like far-flung fiefdoms not doing the emperor's bidding. In other words, our body performs many important, yet almost independent functions subconsciously. Ask anyone how their stomach is digesting food or how their blood pressure is being regulated on a regular day, for example, you will most likely get an oblivious, blank look.

When you throw your hands up in horror, your bodily functions — otherwise quiet little fiefdoms — begin to lose coordination and equilibrium. When panic mode kicks in, the result can be disastrous. We have so often seen sheer stress and anxiety causing athletes to make unbelievably dumb, spectacular errors at competitions.

Yet, it's after all nothing incredulous. Nervousness can indeed be the root of almost all performance errors. When we lose mental and bodily equilibrium, we lose precision in elocution, become skittish, forgetful, inattentive, tongue-tied, and negligent, and act weirdly.... In short, we are at the end of tether, our work error-ridden.

This may sound glum and defeatist to some. They may argue, "By that logic, we'd all be doomed. No matter how well we are prepared, we could be screwed when the all-powerful subconscious acts up and becomes a mess, as we are put to the test." Precisely! That's why we should learn to stay calm under pressure — a mental skill to be honed regularly, so that our mind and body can function well in sync. This after all is far more important than mere smarts.

每个人心中都有一个本子

次我应邀在电台直播，谈些人生感慨什么的，不时有听众的热线打进，大家就聊天。突然，一个很细弱的女声传来，说，毕老师，我有一个本子，不知该怎么办。你能帮我想个主意吗？

我问，什么本子呢？

她说，就是那种老式的本子，每个人年轻的时候，都有那种本子。我想，你也曾有过的。

我的心像古老的张衡发明的地动仪一样，接收到一颗铜球，激烈地共振了一下。我知道她所说的那种本子，我确实有过那种本子。我说，啊，是。我知道，我有过。你打算让我给你出个什么主意呢？

她一口气说下去，不再停歇。看来，她为这个问题，思虑很长时间了。

没有人需要这种本子了，这种本子太老土了。我有时翻翻，也觉得特可笑。却想，可不能把它扔了、烧了，里头藏着我年轻时的梦。多不容易搜集来的呀！我那时用功着呢，别人看电影，我不去，一笔一画地抄呀抄。现在一看，挺幼稚的，可我不忍心把它毁了，心血啊。还抄了不少景物和人物描写，比如《创业史》里，徐改霞的长相，《林海雪原》里，少剑波如何英俊……还有气象谚语，像"天上鲤鱼斑，晒谷不用翻""天上鱼鳞斑，不雨也风颠"……我那时就分辨不清，鲤鱼斑和鱼鳞斑有什么不同？天气好坏能差那么多吗？想了多年，也闹不明白。如今，也不用想了。有了天气预报，什么都简单了。本子还有什么用？再没人需要它了……

我听着，不知如何回应，只有陪着叹息。从她透露的摘抄词，再加上听她的声音，我判断她早已不年轻。有些人生的纪念物，对自己是宝，对他人只是废物。

也许，怀旧的人，可以在自己的家里，建一所微型的历史博物馆？我本想这样说，但一想到这个年纪的中国妇女，一般不惯幽默。不知人家住房是否宽敞，可有这份闲心？要是碰上个下岗女工，反触动了伤心处。于是只有以沉默相伴。

她突然很热切地说，想了很长时间，我决定把本子寄给你。那里面有关文学的描写，对你的写作肯定会有帮助的。

我微微地苦笑了。这种描写，对我不会有实际用处。但这是一个直播节目，我们的对话，已通过电波飞进万千耳朵。我不忍伤害一颗朴素而炽热的心，于是很快地回答说，好啊！谢谢你把这么宝贵的纪念物托付给我，我一定会仔细拜读，妥善保护的。

她接着问了我的工作地址，喃喃地重复着，记录着……其他的电话接踵打进来，她的声音就在鼎沸中淹去了。

几天后，我收到了一个厚厚的包裹，打开来，一个红色的塑料笔记本收入眼底。

果然是逝去年代的遗物。扉页上，盖着洇了红油的公章，不太好的墨字写着"奖给劳动模范×××"。这个笔记本不但有着文学的意义，还是主人光荣的记载。

我细细地翻看本子。字体从稚嫩到圆熟，抄录的内容也形形色色。它不是日记，没有个人生活的流水账，但却能从里面看出生命的过程。除了文艺书籍的片段，更多的是那个时代流传的一些名人名言。抄录者好像不喜欢按部就班地准确记载，有一些话并不注明出处，使人分辨不清是她抄下的，还是自己发明的。

　　在人生的前半，有享乐的能力，而无享乐的机会。在人生的后半，有享乐的机会，而无享乐的能力。

——马克·吐温

　　恕我孤陋寡闻，从来不知马克·吐温有这样一段言论，不知他在何时何地讲的这个话？我虽然很钦佩他老人家的文学成就，但对这段话不敢苟同。我以为，享乐的能力和机会应该是同步的。你用劳动创造机会，同时享乐。把机会和能力割裂开来，大概是20世纪的顺序了。

　　我想，这段话是本子的主人在年轻时抄录下的吧？那时，她肯定以为自己是不应该享乐的。她以这话激励自己。现在，大约她已到了有享乐机会的年纪了，不知她能否安然享乐？

　　一个人专心于本身的时候，他充其量也只能成为一个美丽的、小巧的包裹而已。

——罗斯金

又一次惭愧了，不知这位罗斯金是谁。我从这段话里，猜测到主人是相貌普通的女子。在很长的岁月里，她用这话勉励着自己，不愿做一个美丽、小巧的包裹，而期望是勤奋而努力的战士。

人间最美丽的情景是出现在当我们怀念母亲的时候。

——莫泊桑

这话非常好。主人在这段语录下，画了代表强调意思的曲线。想来，她是一个非常注重亲情的人。她是孝女吧？但也有另一种可能，她从小就失去了母亲。但愿我的后一判断有误。

在最不尊重人类自由的地方，人对英雄的崇拜最为炽烈。

——斯宾塞

人之才能，自非圣贤。有所长，必有所短。有所明，必有所蔽。

——王守仁

当爱情发言的时候，就像诸神的合唱，使整个的天界陶醉于仙乐之中。

——莎士比亚

恋爱中止后不说对方的坏话，也是一种道德。

——国分康孝

"为什么美女总是跟庸庸碌碌的男人结婚？""因为，聪明的男人避开跟美女结婚。"

——毛姆

啊，她这一阶段，在谈恋爱吧？失恋了？

有朋友的人像草原一样广阔，没有朋友的人像手掌一样狭窄。

与邪佞人交，如雪入墨池，虽融为水，其色愈污。与端方人处，如炭入熏炉，虽化为灰，其香不灭。

——此话无出处

每只鸟都认为自己的声音最美。

——阿拉伯谚语

即使把蛇装进竹管里，它也不会因而变直。

——日本谚语

她是否受到了某种伤害？挺过来了吧？

她脚上穿的是一双绣了小蓝花的青布鞋，毛蓝布裤子，红罩衣，浅花头帕下拢着浓密的黑发，黑发在脑后梳成一根油亮亮的粗辫子，粗辫从脑后绕到前边，滑过肩头，垂在富于曲线的胸脯上。辫梢扎了个红毛线的蝴蝶结，身材颀长，体态丰满，一对银耳坠垂在秀丽的脸盘旁……

——人物外貌描写

……

我错落地翻动着本子，无声地读着这些话语，感到一颗心，拖着长长的彗尾，在人生的天际艰难运行。

我很感动，因为自己也有一个这样的本子。从中学时记起，追随我到高原，直至我饱经沧桑。

有一些我们久久蕴积肺腑，却表达不出的心结，被先哲们一语道破，在征途的驿站旁，等着我们路过。当无意间相逢时，心会陡地一颤，紧接着是温暖和相知的潮水涌起。

每个人内心都存着这样的本子，记载着我们尊崇的规则。无论它是否凝结为显形的字迹，都在暗中规定和指挥着我们的思维。

近年，不大有人记这样的本子了。很多人奉行的宗旨，是一些可做却不可说的秘诀。有一个女孩告诉我，她听从这样一些小技巧：

永远别问理发师你是否需要理发。（他总是说你需要理发。推而广之，不要向可能成为你的对手的人、利益与你相悖的人，请教任何东西。）

美貌是一封无声的推荐信，一旦付出，就要成为定期债券。（在出租相貌的时候，一定要计算出到期的收益。蚀本的生意万不可干。）

烧掉自己最难看的照片。

（千万要在第一眼看到之后，就赶快燃起火柴。假装它从来不曾存在过。这会增强自信心。不信，你试试。）

要付的钱晚付，要收的钱早收。

对于狗来说，每一个主人都是拿破仑。

她说，我这些还是比较上得台面的，有的人，干脆只记一句——人不为己，天诛地灭。

我无言。翻看我们心中的本子，会更精练更浓烈地知道我们是怎样的人。

我把红本子珍藏起来。不想一段时间以后，那女子又给我来了一封信，说自从把本子寄给我以后，寝食无安，好像把最珍贵的东西丢了。

真的不是我不相信您，只是我以前没意识到，这本子对我是如此重要。您能把它还给我吗？假如您喜欢其中的某些部分，我可以把它复印了，再给您寄去。我不会要您一分钱的。

我马上把本子挂号寄回并附言。我说，本子我已看完了，对我帮助很大。不必再印了。非常感谢你。我完全能理解你的情感，因为我也有同样的本子。

又过了些日子，我收到了厚厚的邮包。打开来看，那女子把她的笔记本，工工整整地重抄了一份，给我寄来了。

后面多了一句话，没有写明出处，我不知是她自己杜撰的，还是从哪里抄来的。

当你全心全意梦想着什么的时候，整个宇宙都会协同起来，助你实现自己的心愿。

That Little Notebook in Every Heart

Once I was on live radio, talking about life itself, now and then interrupted by calls from the audience, and then we would chat a little. As the program went on, suddenly, a woman's voice, weak and low, was heard, saying: "Dear Miss Bi, I have a notebook, but I don't know what to do with it. You have any idea?" I asked her to be more specific. She explained that it was old-fashioned, the sort that everybody seemed to have owned a copy when they were young. "Yourself included," she added.

My heart gave a leap, like the mobile celestial globe invented by Zhang Heng — having received a copper ball, it gave a violent leap. I know the kind of notebook that she was talking about, and I had indeed owned one. I answered, "I know the kind that you are talking about. I had owned one myself. What do you want me to advise you about?"

She started talking non-stop, obviously having already pondered over the problem.

"No one uses this kind of notebook anymore, as it is so old-fashioned. I flip through it now and then and can't help laughing. But then I remind myself that I must on no account burn it — it contains the dreams of my youth. I was so studious at the time. When everybody else went off to the movies, I would stay put and copy quotations into my notebook. Looking back, it was childish, but I still cannot bring myself to destroy it. The notebook is my lifeblood. I had also copied down descriptions of people and of sceneries. Take, for instance, the description of the heroine Xu Gaixia in the novel *How We Built Our Life Together*, or the description of the handsome hero Shao Jianbo in *A Sea of Forests and A Wilderness of Snow*. And then there were idioms in weather lore such as 'carp spots cloud in the sky, good weather to make grain dry,' or 'fish scales cloud in the sky, either rain or wind.' At the time I was confused about the different kinds of fish scales cloud, and was sceptical about the way that weather was supposed to be affected by them. I had always wondered but was never able to decipher the different kinds of fish scales and just gave up trying. And now that we have the weather forecast, everything is made easier. The notebook had outlived its usefulness and no one cared..."

I listened to the woman's story, but did not know how to respond and just kept sighing in sympathy. To judge from the quotations that she had picked and the sound of her voice, I could tell that she was no longer young and did have some keepsakes that were precious to her alone, but trash to the unconcerned.

Perhaps the nostalgic folks should set up a

mini historic museum for themselves in their own home? I had wanted to raise the issue. Then I remembered that Chinese women of that age were lacking in humour as a rule. Who knows if they owned that kind of space, and whether they were in the mood. If she happened to be one of those who had been laid off from the workplace, her feelings would be hurt. So I remained silent.

Suddenly her voice rang out, saying, "After some hard thinking, I have decided to mail the notebook to you. There are some literary flourishes in there, and it may be helpful for your writing."

I forced a smile. The kind of jottings in her notebook would serve no useful purpose for me. But this was a live broadcast, and our conversation had already penetrated thousands of ears. I was certainly not going to hurt her feelings in front of a live audience. I answered promptly, "Good! Thank you for leaving with me such a valuable keepsake. I will read it, and I will keep it safe." She then asked me for my work address, writing it down as she repeated the words after me.

Meanwhile, other phone calls came buzzing in, and her voice was lost in the general excitement.

A couple of days later, I received a bulging bag through the mail. As I opened it, a notebook in a red plastic cover met my eyes, obviously an out-dated piece of goods, with a red stamp on the front page and a few words of dedication in shaky calligraphy: "For the model worker XXX." So this red notebook was not only of literary value for the owner, but was also a witness of her honour in the workplace.

I flipped through the pages, the handwriting evolving from childish to mature, and the notes taken down covered a wide range. It was not a diary, nor a record of daily happenings, though you could feel life throbbing between the lines. There were passages from famous publications, but in greater numbers were quotations from notable figures in history. The note taker seems to have taken liberties with the text and omitted the source, so that sometimes one could not tell whether the passage was a quote, or one of the note taker's own concoction.

> It is the epitome of life. The first half of life consists of the capacity to enjoy without the chance; the last half consists of the chance without the capacity.
>
> — Mark Twain (1835 – 1910)

Please forgive my ignorance. I had never come across this statement by Mark Twain. I wonder where and when he made such a statement. I have great respect for his literary achievements but cannot agree with his statement. To me, the capacity and the opportunity to enjoy life go hand in hand: you create the opportunity through labour and you enjoy the labour of creation. I think it is the twentieth century that created the split between the two.

I guess that the above quote had been copied down when the owner of the notebook was young. At the time, she probably considered herself as undeserving of fun and games, and had encouraged herself by such statements as the quotation above. By now, she has probably reached the age for fun and games. I wonder if she has seized the opportunity and been at ease with pleasure.

A man wrapped up in himself makes a very small parcel.

— John Ruskin (1819 — 1900)

This is a case for my embarrassment — I have no idea who is this Ruskin. To judge from this statement my guess is that he was an ordinary young man, and over the years had used this statement to encourage himself not to be a pretty little bundle but to be a warrior.

The most beautiful facial expression in the world appears at the moment when we are thinking of our mother.

— Guy de Maupassant, (1850 — 1899)

177

Well said indeed. The owner of the notebook had underlined this statement. Obviously she herself had strong family ties. Was she a dutiful daughter? There is another possibility — she had lost her mother in childhood. I hope that I am wrong on the last count.

Hero worship is strongest where there is least regard for human freedom.

— Herbert Spencer (1820 — 1903)

People's talents are not God-given. Strength in one area is certain to be matched by weakness in another.

— Wang Shouren (1472 — 1529)

And when love speaks, the voice of all the gods makes Heaven drowsy with the harmony.

— William Shakespeare (1564 — 1606)

When love is gone, do not speak ill of your "ex". It is a moral issue.

— Yasutaka Kokubu (1930 —)

"Why do beautiful women always marry boring men?"

"Because smart men avoid beautiful women."

— William Somerset Maugham (1874 — 1965)

Has she fallen in love lately? And disappointed in love?

People with friends have broadened out, like the boundless grasslands.

People without friends are narrowed down like the palm of your hand.

Dealing with sinister people, is like snow mixed with dirt. Although turning to water, it is still murky. In the company of upright people, they are like charcoal in the oven — although reduced to ashes, their warmth lingers on.

— Author unknown

Every bird thinks its own chirp the sweetest.

— Arabian proverb

Even if stuffed into a segment of bamboo, the snake will not straighten itself out.

— Japanese proverb

Has she been hurt? Has she gotten over it?

Her feet were stuffed into handmade shoes embroidered with blue flowers. She wore cotton trousers dyed blue, and a red top.

Her jet black hair, braided, swung around her shoulders and glided down her breast, ending in a knot of red ribbon. Tall she stood, a pair of silver earrings dangling down either side of her cheeks.

— Notes on figure appearance

I flipped through the pages, silently going over the words, and sensed that a solitary heart was struggling alone, like a comet dragging its tail across the universe. I was very moved, because I myself had owned a notebook like this one. It had followed me from high school all the way to the highlands, witnessing all my ups and downs.

Sometimes, we are stuck for a word to express what we had been brooding over. Then, we chance upon a quote by an earlier writer that captures it perfectly and is there all the time waiting for us as we journey through life. Our heart skips a beat and a warm feeling of finding a kindred spirit fills our entire being.

There is such a little notebook in every heart, inscribed, in legible script or otherwise, with the rules that we revere, mandating and directing our thinking.

Nowadays, few still keep such a notebook. Many follow unspoken rules that are better left hidden. I was told by a girl about such little tricks that she would practice:

— Never ask a hairstylist if you need a trim. (He will invariably urge you to have one. In other words, never seek advice from a potential opponent or adversary.)

— Beauty can open doors for you. Use it to your advantage. (That is: with wise calculation and avoid any unprofitable transaction.)

— Burn any photo of yourself that you detest. (Best do it as soon as you see them. Pretend they have never existed. This will boost your self-confidence. Try it and you will know.)

— Pay what you owe others as late as possible and collect what you are owed as early as possible.

— To every dog, its master is a Napoleon.

The girl added that these rules of hers were quite respectable. She knew others who only believed in "Every man for himself and the Devil takes the hindmost."

I was speechless. We acquire more insight of ourselves as we flip through the little notebooks in our heart.

I put away the red notebook. Sometime later, a letter from that woman arrived unexpectedly in the mail. In it, she wrote that she had felt restless after sending me her old notebook, as if she had lost her most valuable possession. She added that it was not that she did not trust me, but that she had not realized that the notebook was of such importance to her. "Could you return the notebook to me?" she asked. "I could make a photocopy of any pages that you liked and mail it to you at no cost to you."

I sent her notebook back at once through registered mail, with a note saying that, "I enjoyed reading through your notebook and found it very helpful. Your offer is much appreciated, but there is no need to make a photocopy. I fully understand how you feel for I have a similar notebook myself."

Still sometime later, I received a bulging bag through the mail. She had sent me a replica of her notebook, copied by hand in neat handwriting, with one more quote on the last page. I do not know if it was written up by herself or she had got it from somewhere. It reads:

> When you dream of something wholeheartedly, the universe will work in your favour.